THE BIG YELLOW DRAWING BOOK

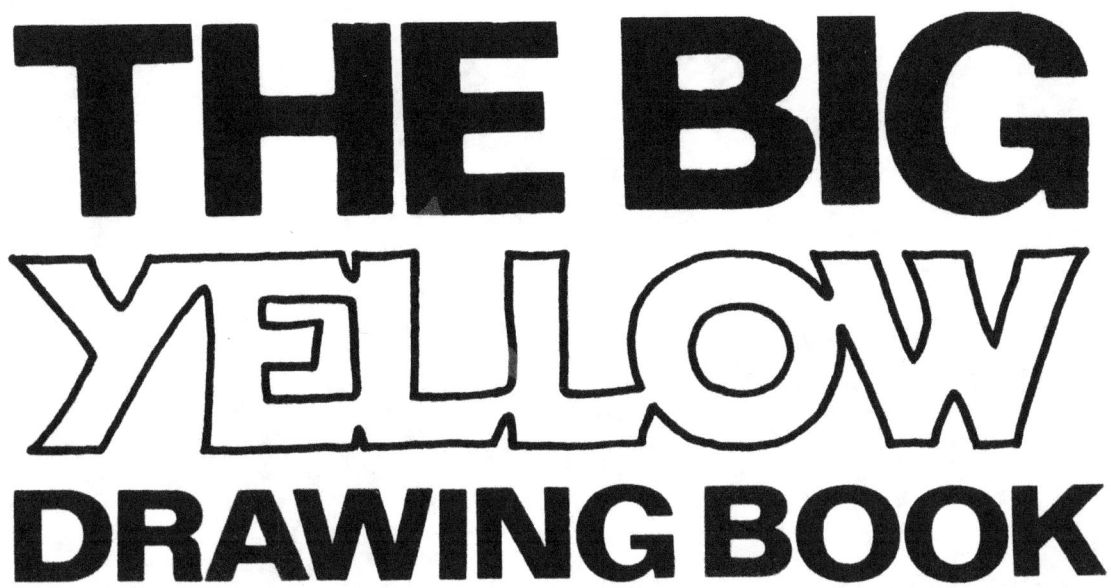

a workbook emphasizing the basic principles of learning, teaching and drawing through cartooning

BY
DAN O'NEILL
MARIAN O'NEILL
HUGH D. O'NEILL JR.

ISBN-13: 978-0615763484 (Hugh Daniel O'Neill III)

ISBN-10: 0615763480

Seventh Printing
Hugh O'Neill and Associates
Nevada City California 95959

www.bydb.com
Printed in the United States of America

introduction

This is a different drawing book. It is based upon a programmed approach to learning and the conviction that anyone who doodles can draw. This does not mean that doodlers will suddenly become famous cartoonists or artists. It does mean that anyone can draw well enough for their own purposes and pleasure.

The book is different in another area. It presents the concept that drawing is a basis of fine art and that the basic principles of good drawing have been defined. Because these principles have been defined they must be learned if a three-dimensional illusion is to be presented on a two-dimensional piece of paper.

In developing the book a suspicion arose that the un-definable mysticism of art should be rejected. The tired old concept that discovery is the only approach to art is considered inefficient. Under this concept it is generally held that a person will make five thousand errors in learning to draw.

The problem here is that there is no assurance that five thousand is the limit. There are an infinite number of ways to do something wrong as compared to a relatively few ways to do something right. It is less time consuming to learn a definable few with direction, than to discover the same few after wading through an infinite number of errors. The ideal is held that satisfactory drawing can be learned without making a single error. That this is an ideal and would seldom occur in fact does not deny the concept.

These concepts were tested in the most difficult of all arenas: The Market Place. In both rural and metropolitan school settings students from kindergarten through high school were presented the material. Several grandmothers, one an eighty-year old, along with all available pre-school great-grandchildren were given the material. Students in two Universities and teachers in three workshops were exposed. In all more than two hundred and ninety-seven people in various settings were volunteer students. From the beginning the response was predicted to be favorable. What was not predicted was the magnitude of the favorable response. Where something like eighty-five percent was considered possible, the ninety-nine percent achieved was extremely rewarding.

Several of the teachers took the material into their classes with the same results.

Why?

This question opens an infinite number of gates, any one of which can lead to the right road, or depending upon the viewpoint, the wrong road. The why in these cases is defined as programmed success for teacher and student. Obviously, no pre-school youngster will be able to read all of the vocabulary running through the instructions… but a teacher or parent can. Helping a youngster in these cases is rewarding especially if a person can see the youngster develop. The presentation was designed that in the early ages, pre-school and primary grade levels, adult help is required. With this help, the youngsters succeed. They like the results, and the parent or teacher cannot help but catch their enthusiasm. A note of caution here. The work of the youngster does not have to be perfect. The child does not have to draw a perfect circle. Any approximation is acceptable. No single individual's work is better or worse than any other individual's work. Individual interpretation of success is sufficient. The child will develop more expert capability with practice and time providing practice is continued. Practice will more likely continue if sugar is given in the form of smiles or kind words, rather thank giving vinegar in the form of criticism and frowns.

This is the psychological law of effect, which in general states that a person will more likely repeat actions which are rewarding than those which are not rewarding. For a youngster a reasonably sure reward is teacher or parent acceptance of something he feels he has done well.

For older students and adults, the principles are presented in such a sequence that self-recognized success is as close to certainty as possible. Obviously some will have more time to give than others. But this is not the point. Each principle is within the capability of any reasonably normal person. The reward for these individuals is the self-recognized progress. How much mastery an individual desires depends upon the person and the time available for practice. At the end of the last lesson an individual will draw better than at the end of the first lesson and will have a feeling that expertise in drawing is only a matter of practice. Again a note of caution. *Do not skip exercises. Each succeeding exercise depends upon the preceding exercise.* An assumption of success is not the same as achieving success. For most of us an assumption or even certainty does not generate the same pleasant feeling as actual achievement. A goal of the book for older students and adults is the generation of this "good feeling" along with recognized mastery at a personal level. This "good feeling" is the thing that is most likely to motivate a person into going on to more sophisticated mastery.

To go back to the question 'why." The book is psychologically sound. It is carefully designed from the simple to the complex. The emotional need for success is recognized in progressive, possible achievement. The basic principles for successful drawing are recognized and presented. Self-discovery, which is not necessarily instruction, is left for later, after the individual has learned the basic skills.

To put it more plainly, the book is designed around Grandmother's concept that more flies are caught with sugar than vinegar, and around mother's concept that patience and work can result in success.

Based upon these principles, if an individual picks up a pencil and completes the first couple of exercises, he will convince himself that anyone can draw, can feel good about drawing and should draw.

Hugh D. O'Neill, Jr.
Ed.D. Educational Psychology
University of Oklahoma, 1969
Counselor Education
University of San Francisco

HI,

SO YOU DON'T THINK YOU CAN DRAW CARTOONS..? WELL.. IF YOU CAN WRITE THE ALPHABET, SIGN YOUR NAME, AND SEE SIX INCHES **YOU** CAN DRAW CARTOONS!

ALL CARTOONS ARE **SIGNALS**.. EXACTLY THE WAY STOP SIGNS, RED LIGHTS, GREEN LIGHTS ARE SIGNALS. SIGNALS GIVE US **INFORMATION**.. STOP, GO..SLOW DOWN..

THE CARTOON CHARACTER HAS A SIGNAL ON ITS FACE.. AN **EXPRESSION**! THIS EXPRESSION TELLS US THE CHARACTER IS **FEELING** AN **EMOTION**. THE WAY OUR CHARACTER **LOOKS** TELLS US WHAT IT **FEELS** .. AND THAT TELLS US **MUCH** MORE THAN THE WORDS THE CHARACTER WILL SPEAK.

THE SIGNALS ARE SIMPLE. GET YOURSELF A SOFT LEAD **DARK** PENCIL AND TURN THE PAGE... ⟹

" HELLO.. THIS IS THE VOICE OF YOUR **CARTOON** SPEAKING.. YOU ARE GOING TO DRAW ME.. START BY DRAWING A **BIG CIRCLE** IN THE NEXT PANEL..."

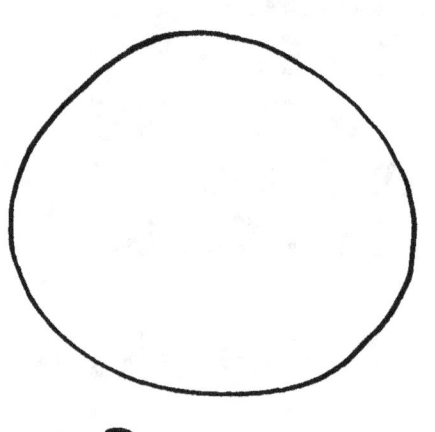

.. A BIG CIRCLE ..

" THIS CIRCLE IS THE BEGINNING OF MY **FACE** !! NOW I NEED **EYES**.. SO DRAW TWO LITTLE CIRCLES **CLOSE** TOGETHER IN THE TOP HALF OF THE BIG CIRCLE.."

" .. ADD SOME BIG DOTS IN THE LITTLE CIRCLES.. AND I HAVE **EYEBALLS**.. NOW I CAN SEE.. DRAW EYES AND EYEBALLS IN ALL THE CIRCLES ON THIS PAGE.."

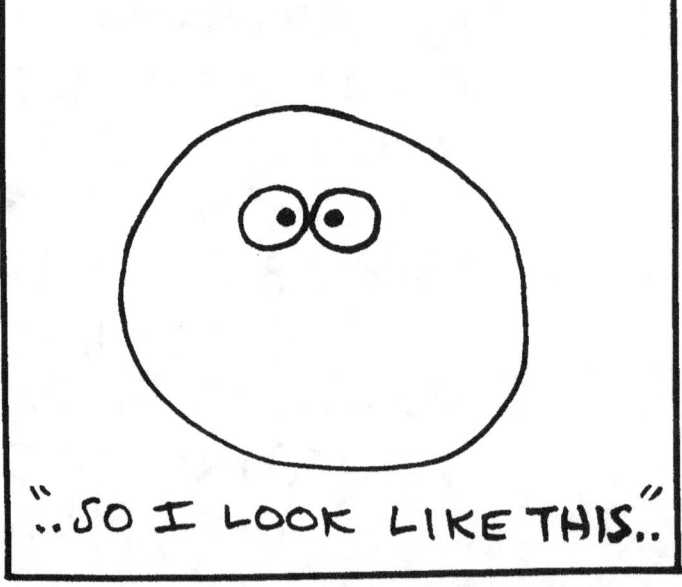

".. SO I LOOK LIKE THIS.."

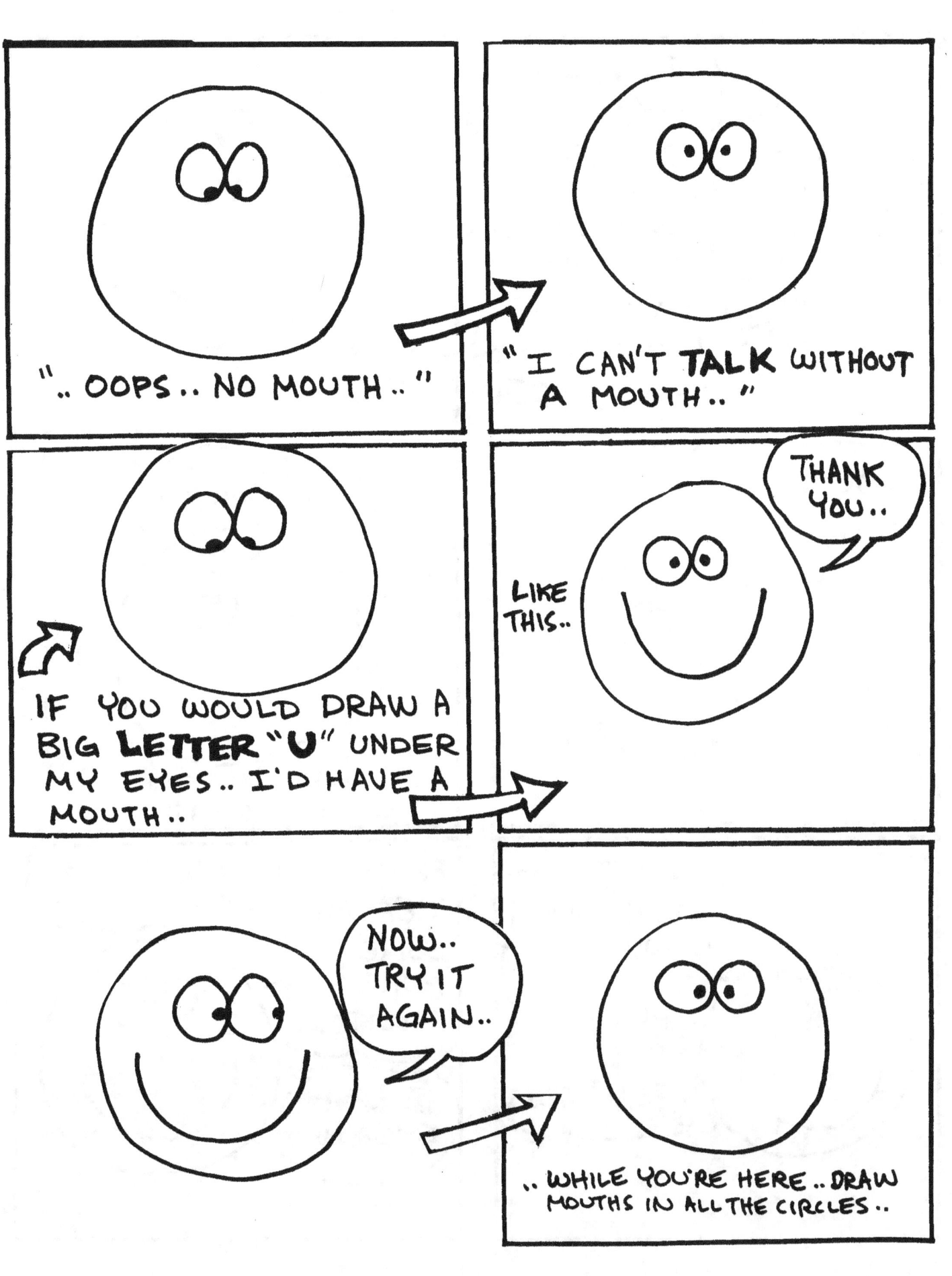

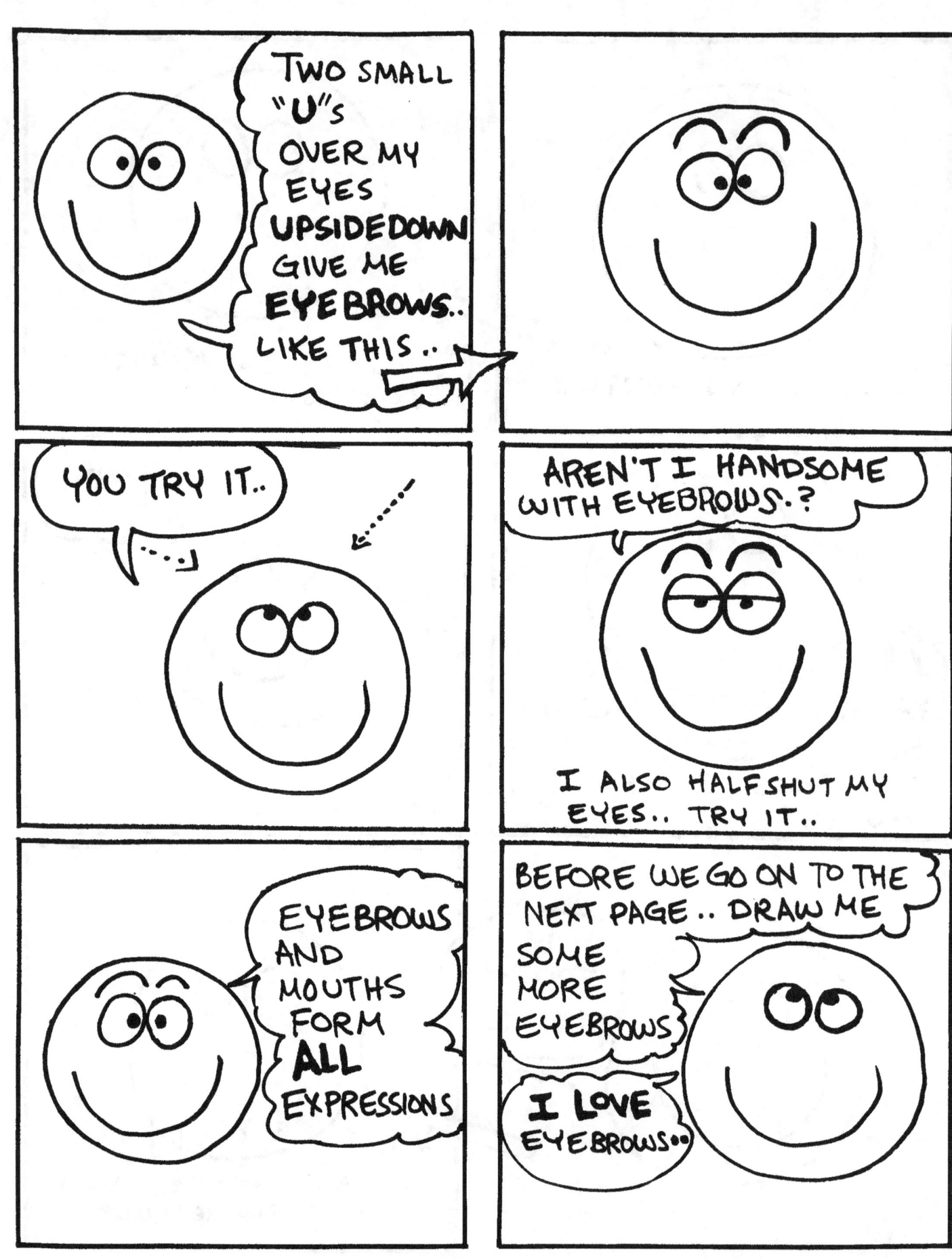

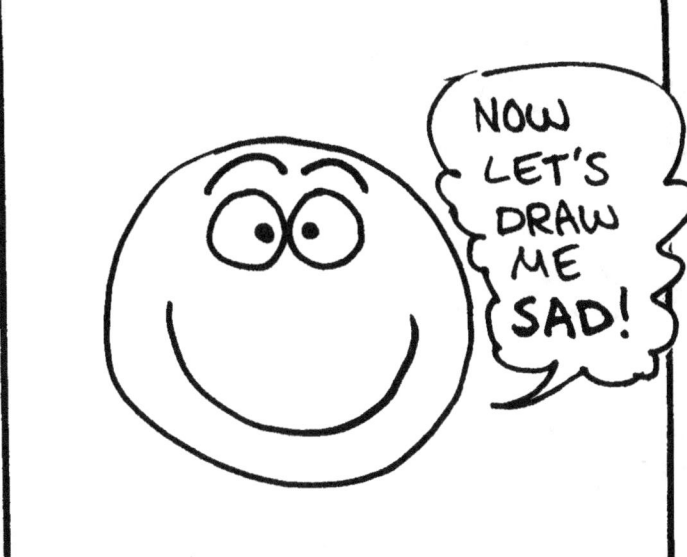

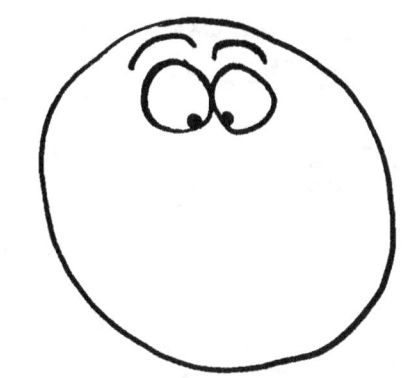

DRAW THE BIG LETTER "U" UPSIDEDOWN..

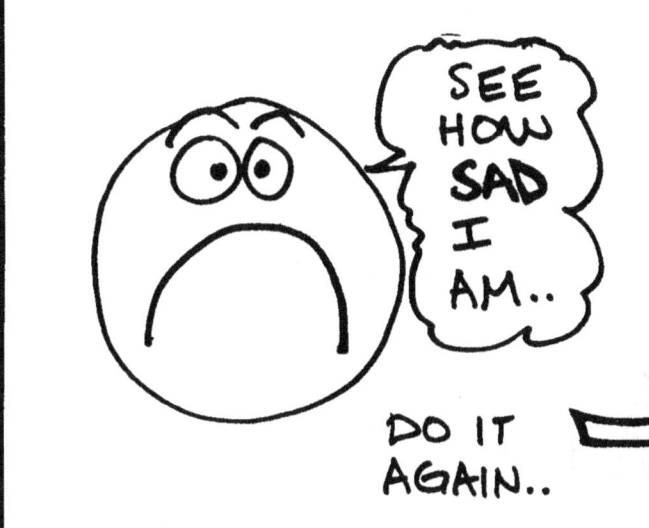

DO IT AGAIN..

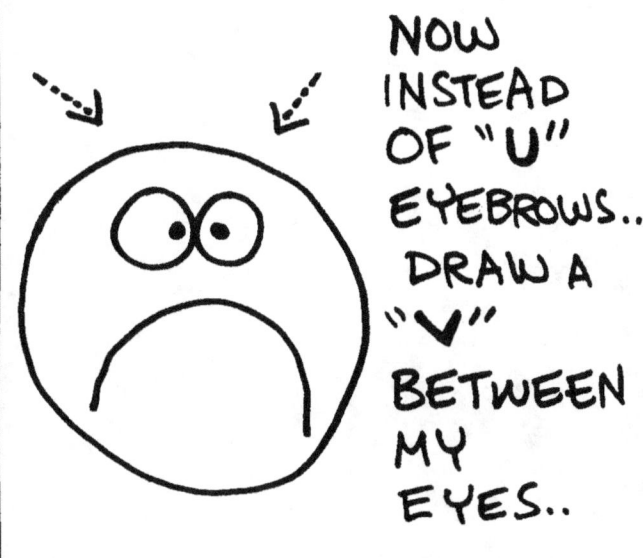

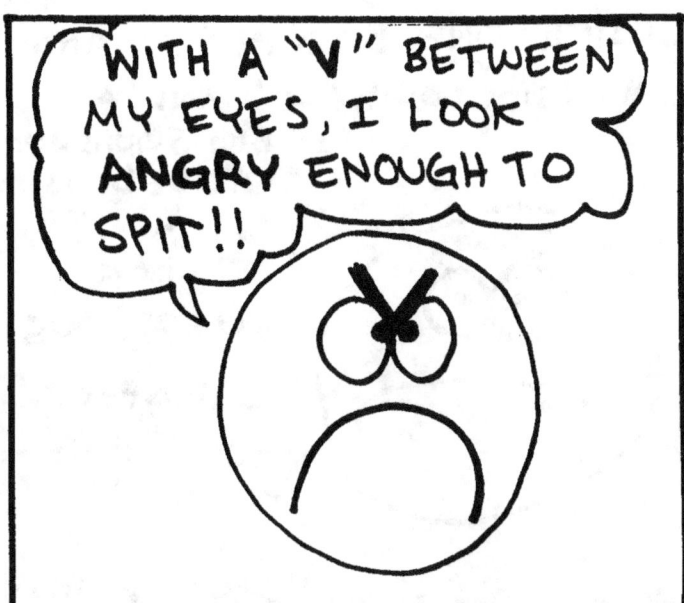

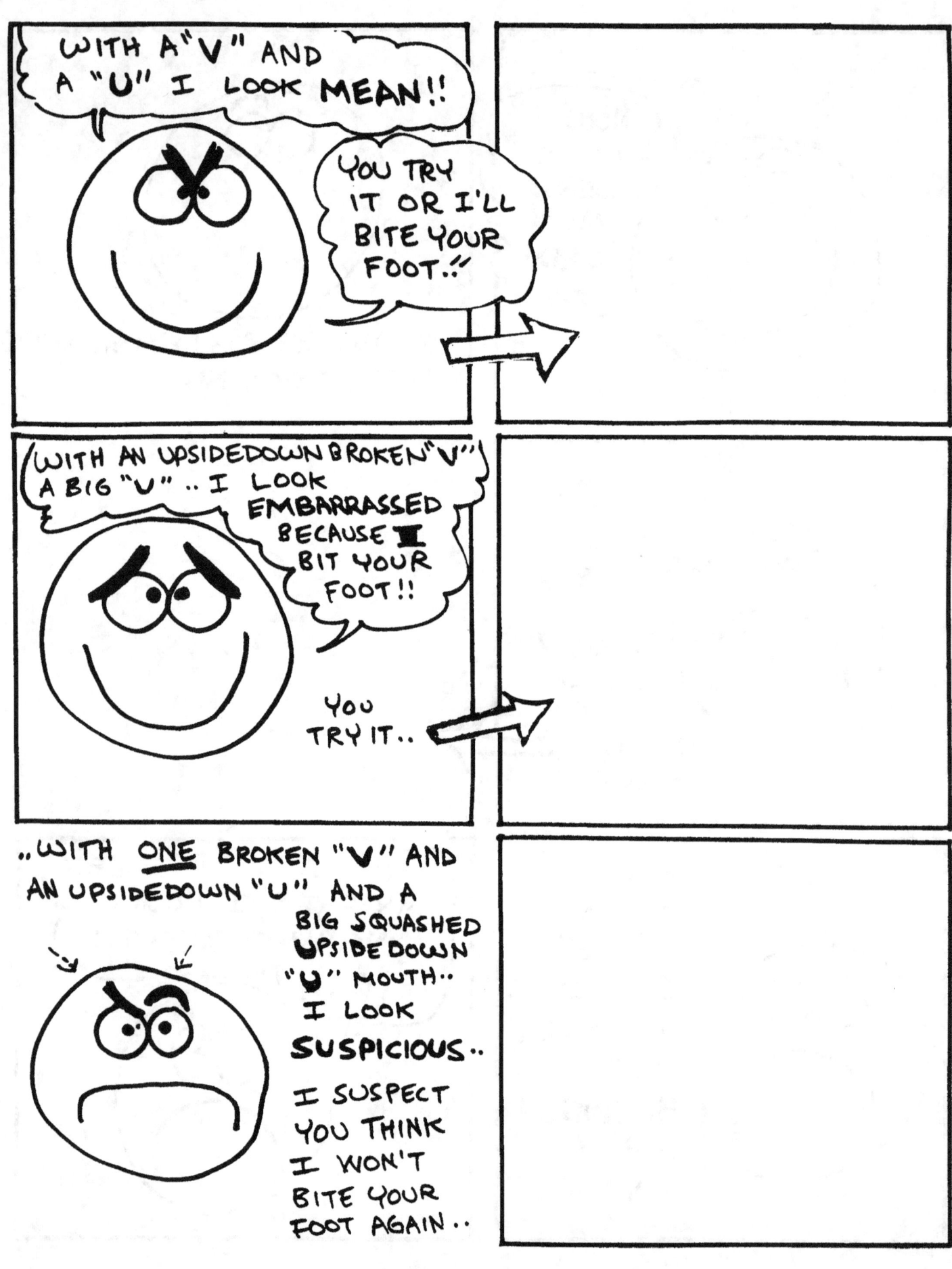

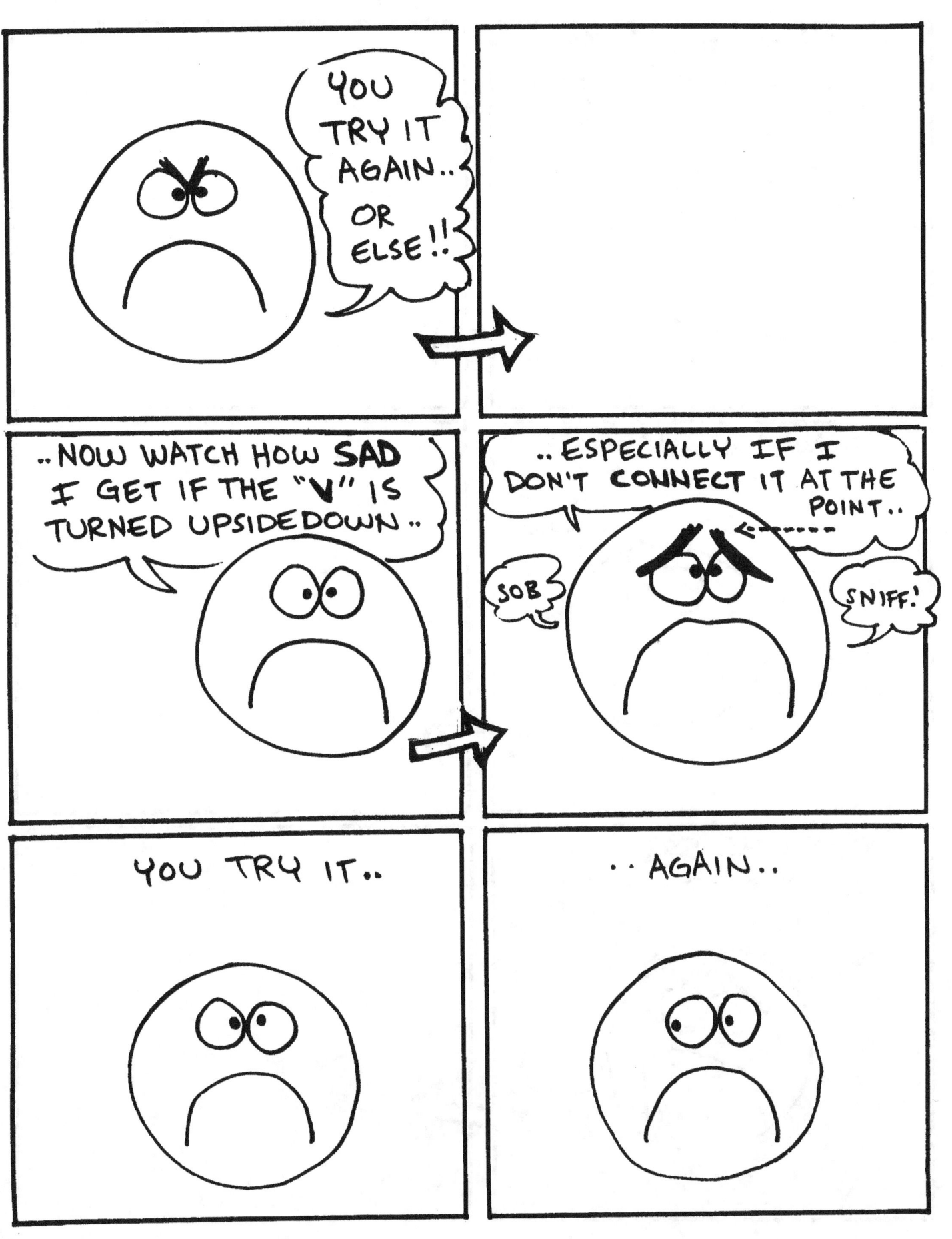

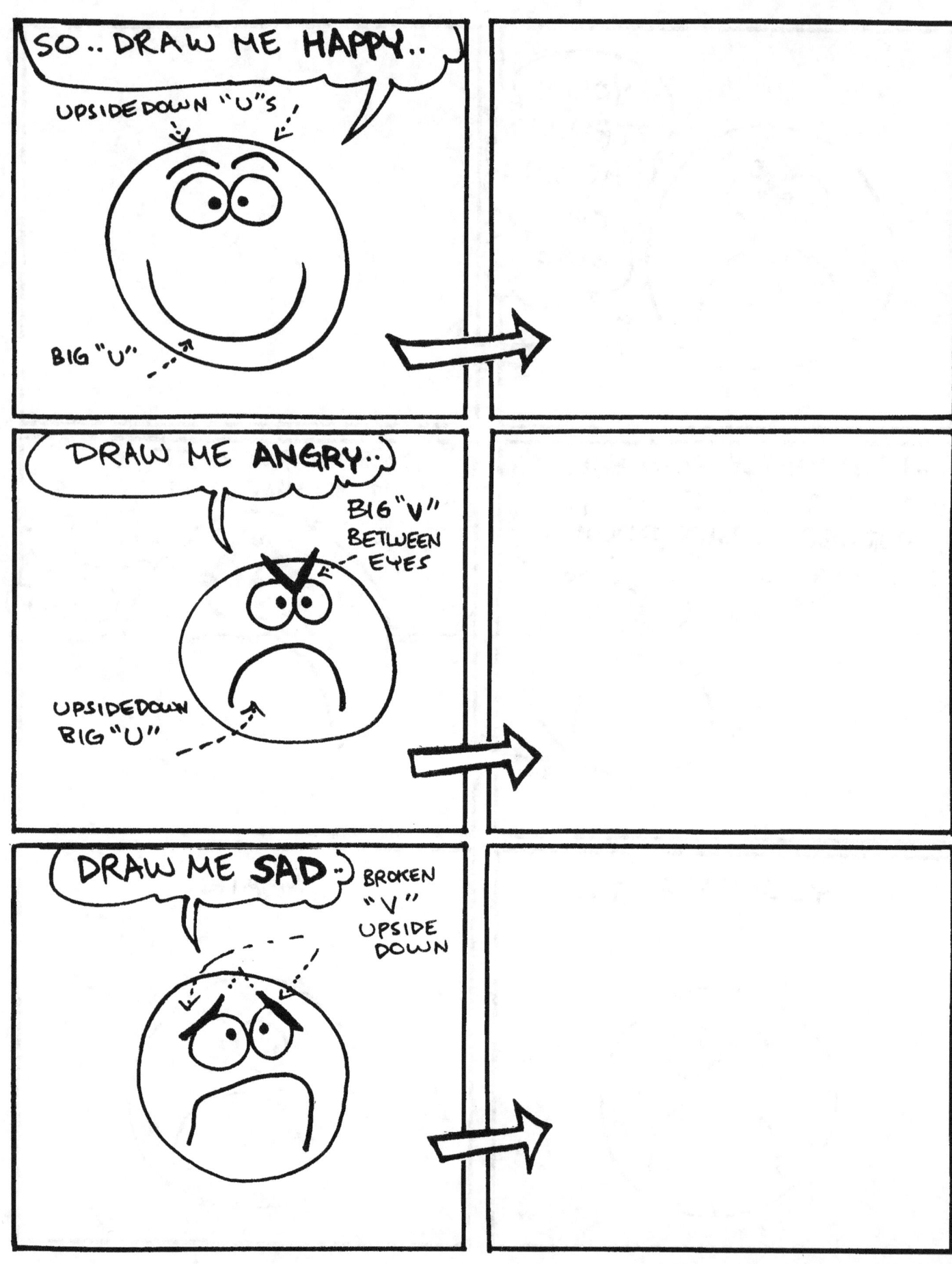

ADDING EYELIDS CHANGES THE EMOTION!

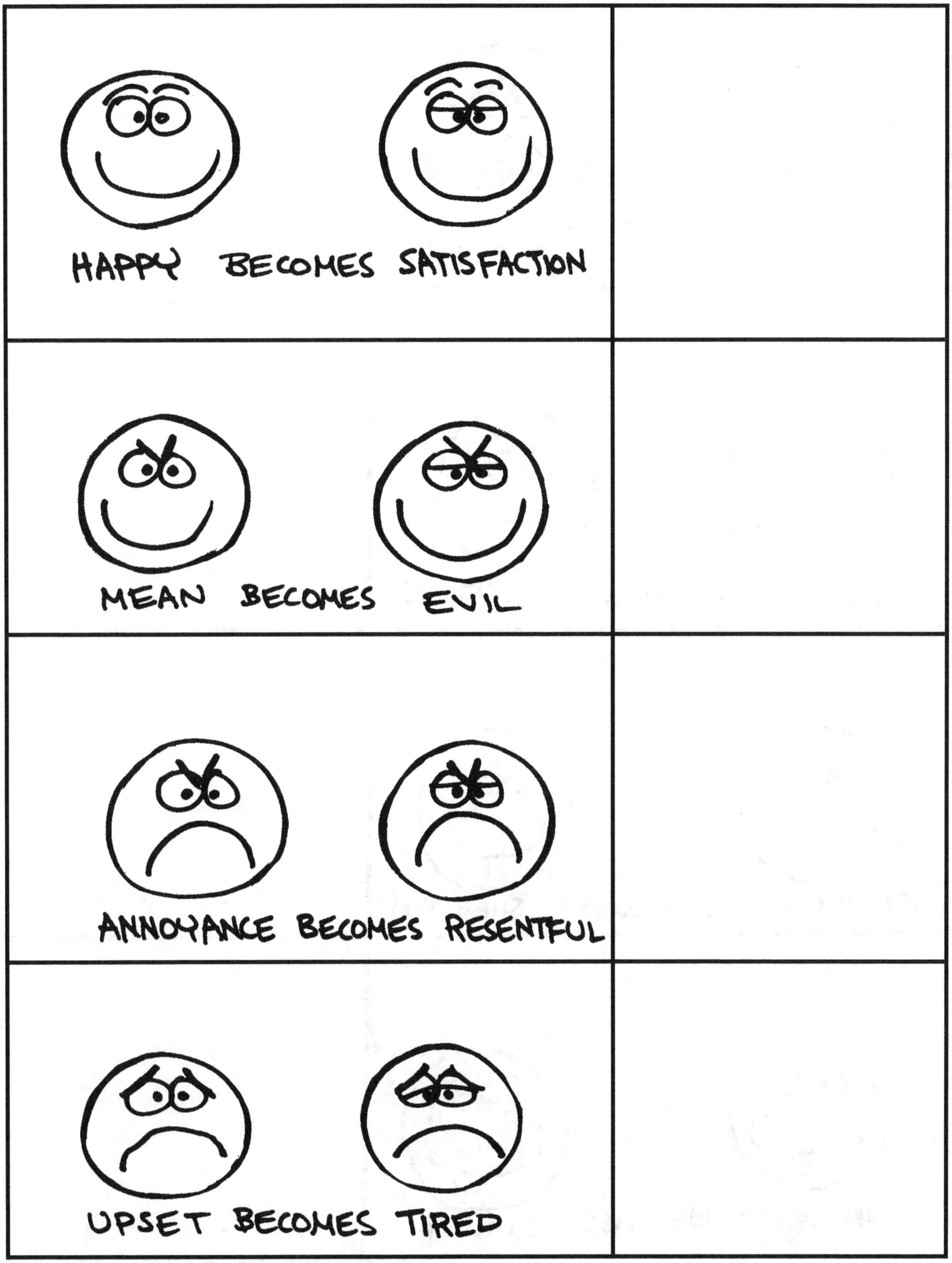

HAPPY BECOMES SATISFACTION

MEAN BECOMES EVIL

ANNOYANCE BECOMES RESENTFUL

UPSET BECOMES TIRED

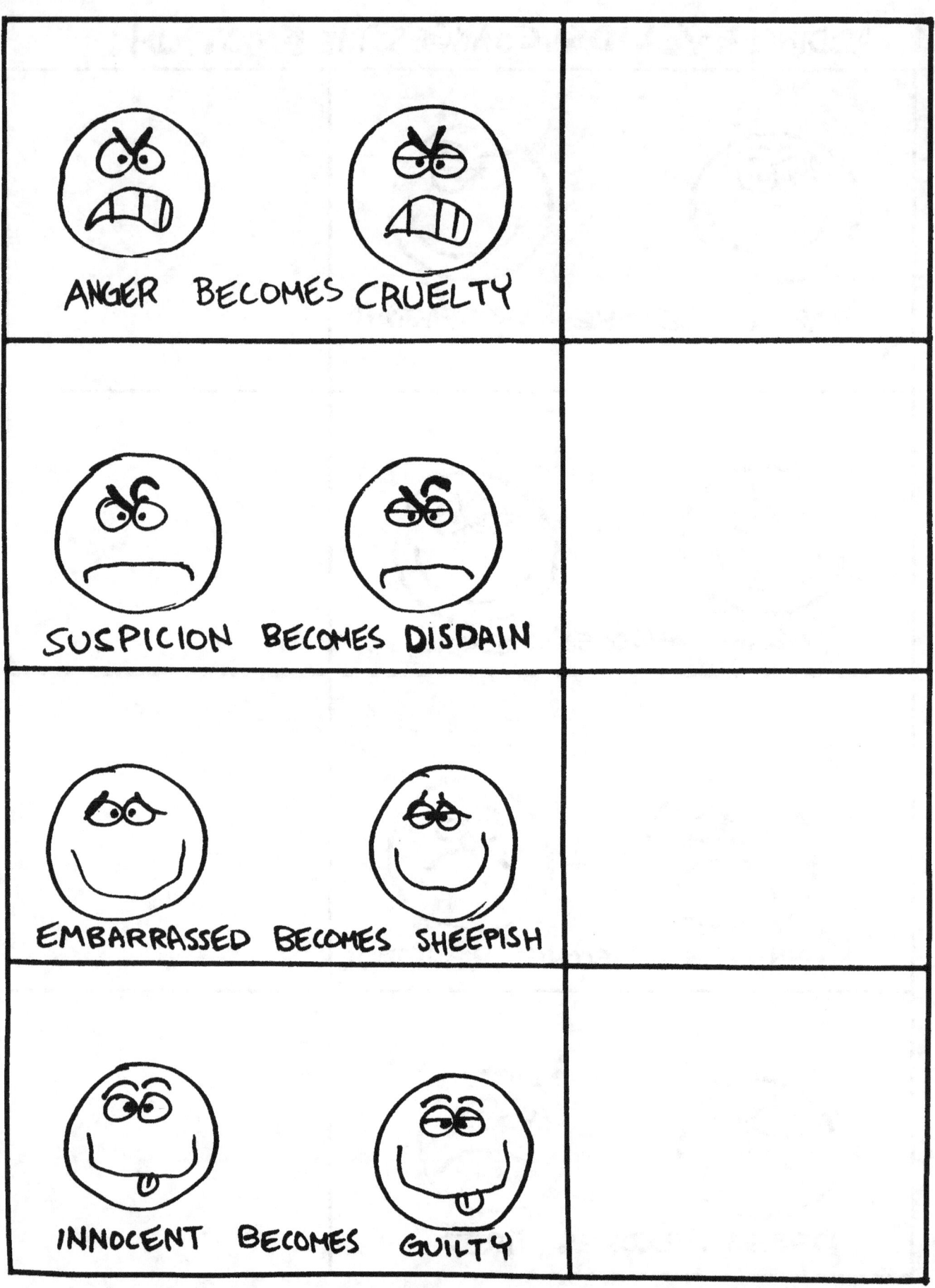

WE ADD PERSPECTIVE TO OUR DRAWING TO GAIN THE **ILLUSION** OF THREE DIMENSIONS.... HEIGHT, WEIGHT AND VOLUME .!! THE FIRST PRINCIPLE IS **SIZE**!

I AM DRAWN LARGER HERE SO I APPEAR CLOSER TO YOU..

THE ILLUSION OF DISTANCE BETWEEN US IS CREATED BY SIZE!

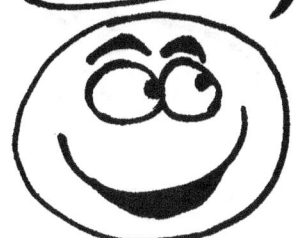

THE SMALLER I AM .. THE FARTHER AWAY I AM FROM YOU..

THE BIGGER I GET..

THE CLOSER I AM..

DRAW US IN THE SPACE BELOW..

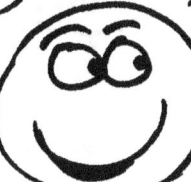
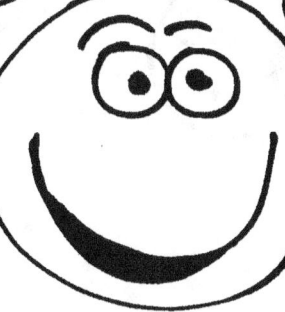

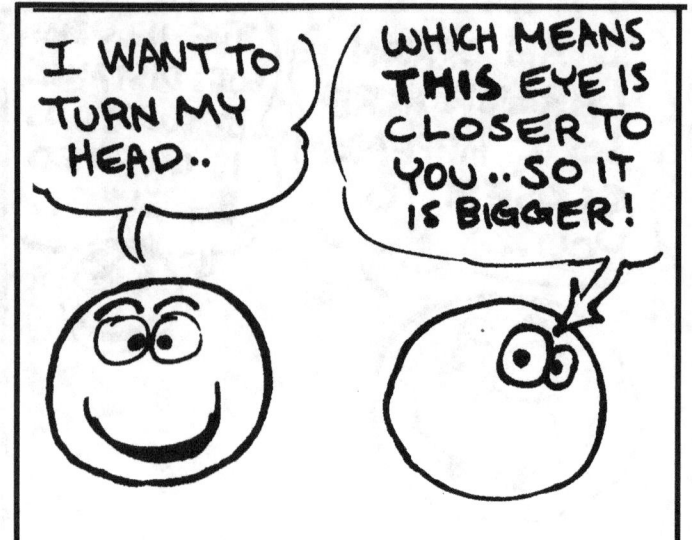

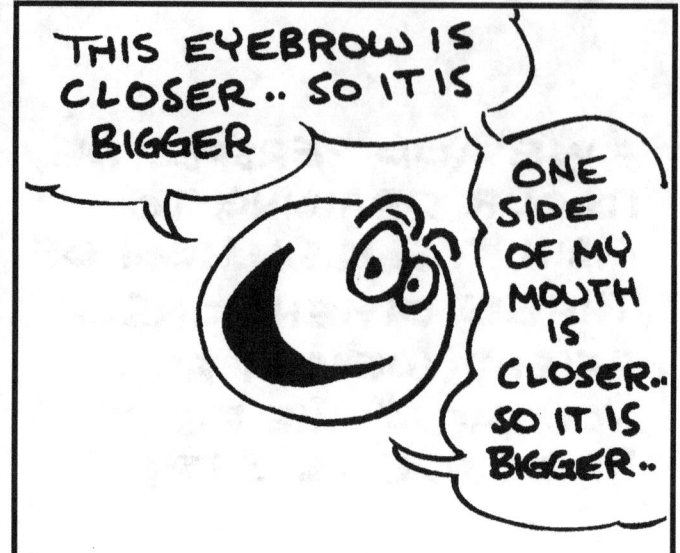

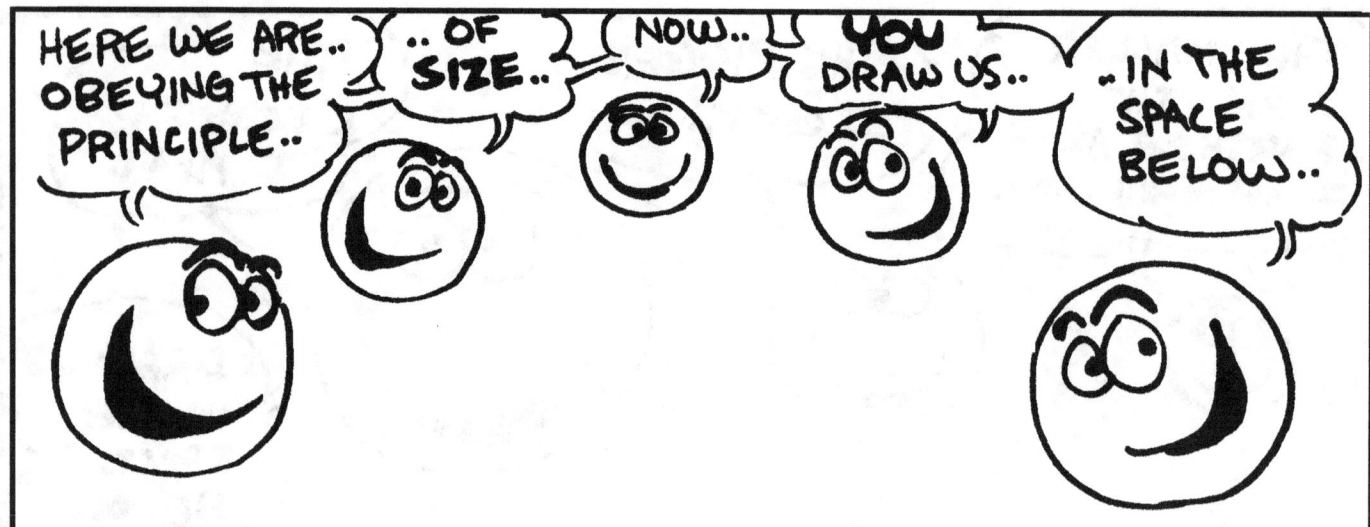

REMEMBER.. ALL PARTS OF MY FACE CLOSEST TO YOU ARE DRAWN LARGER..

THE SECOND PRINCIPLE OF PERSPECTIVE — OVERLAPPING!

OVERLAPPING ADDED TO SIZE **DEEPENS** THE ILLUSION OF DIMENSION..

ALL OF THESE PRINCIPLES WORK AS A **TEAM** TO PRODUCE THIS ILLUSION!

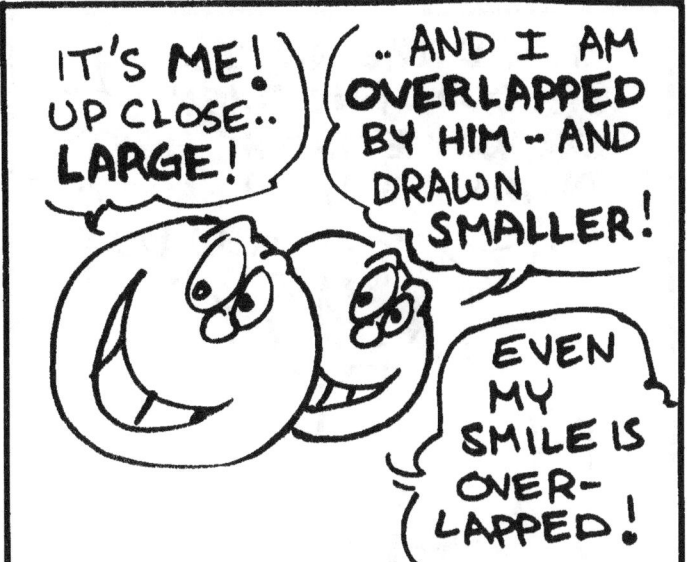

IT'S ME! UP CLOSE.. **LARGE!**

.. AND I AM **OVERLAPPED** BY HIM -- AND DRAWN **SMALLER!**

EVEN MY SMILE IS OVER-LAPPED!

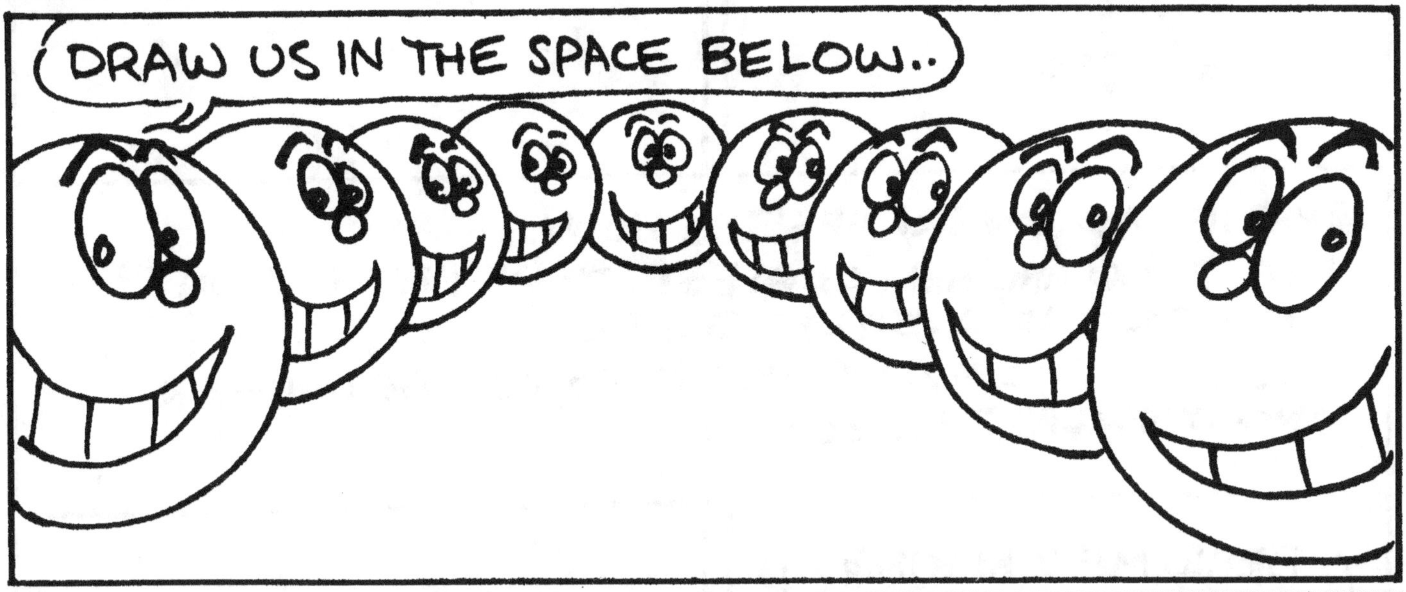

DRAW US IN THE SPACE BELOW..

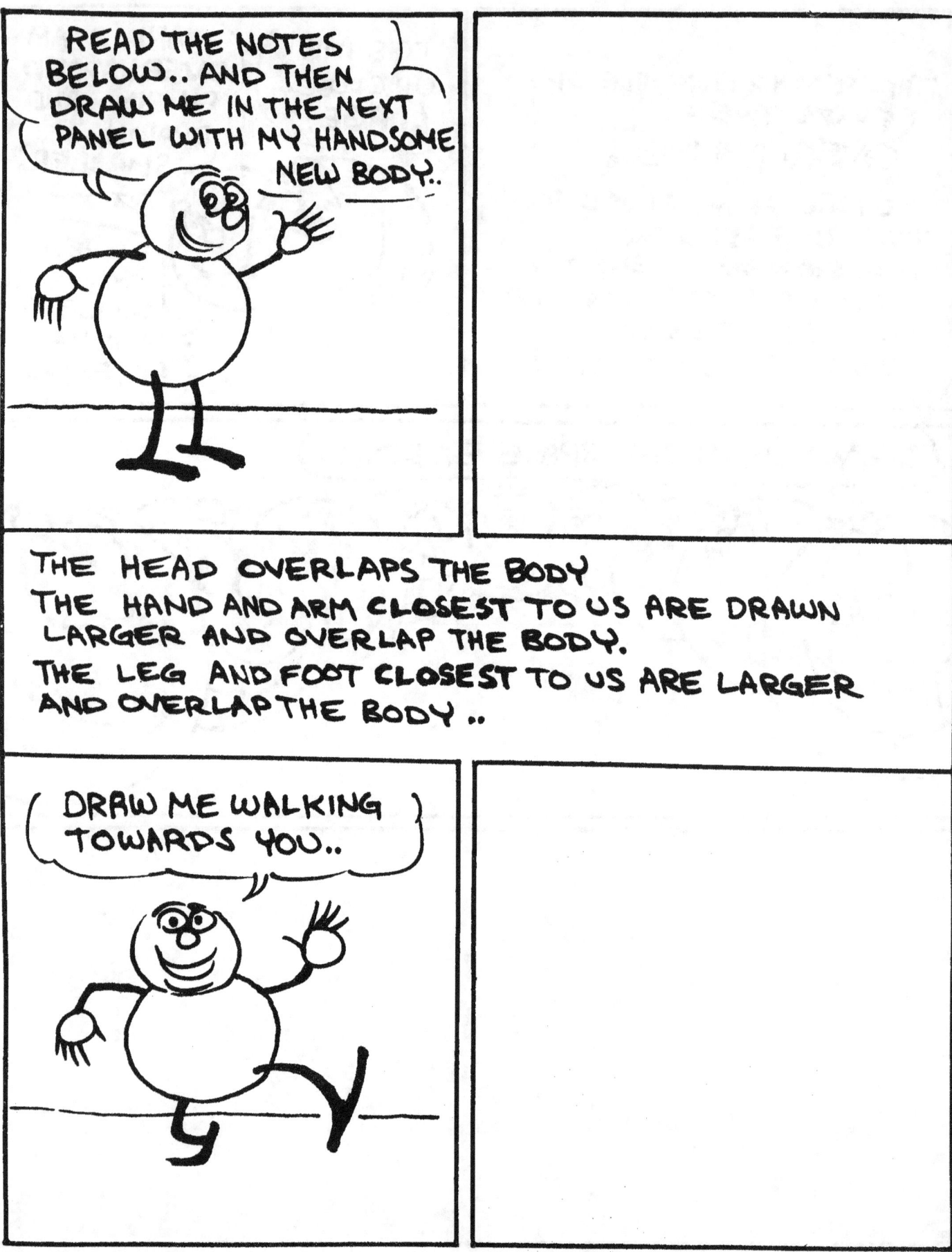

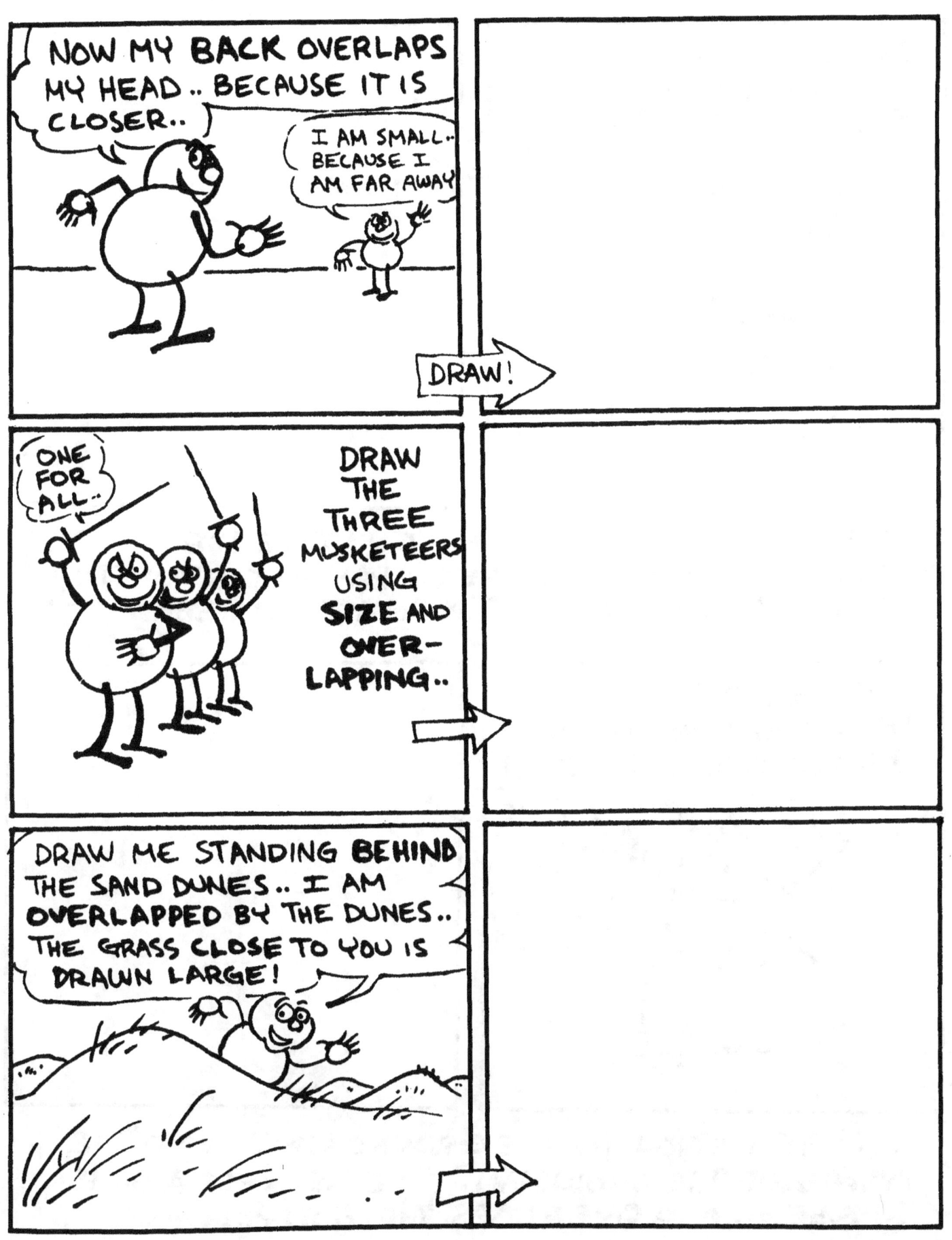

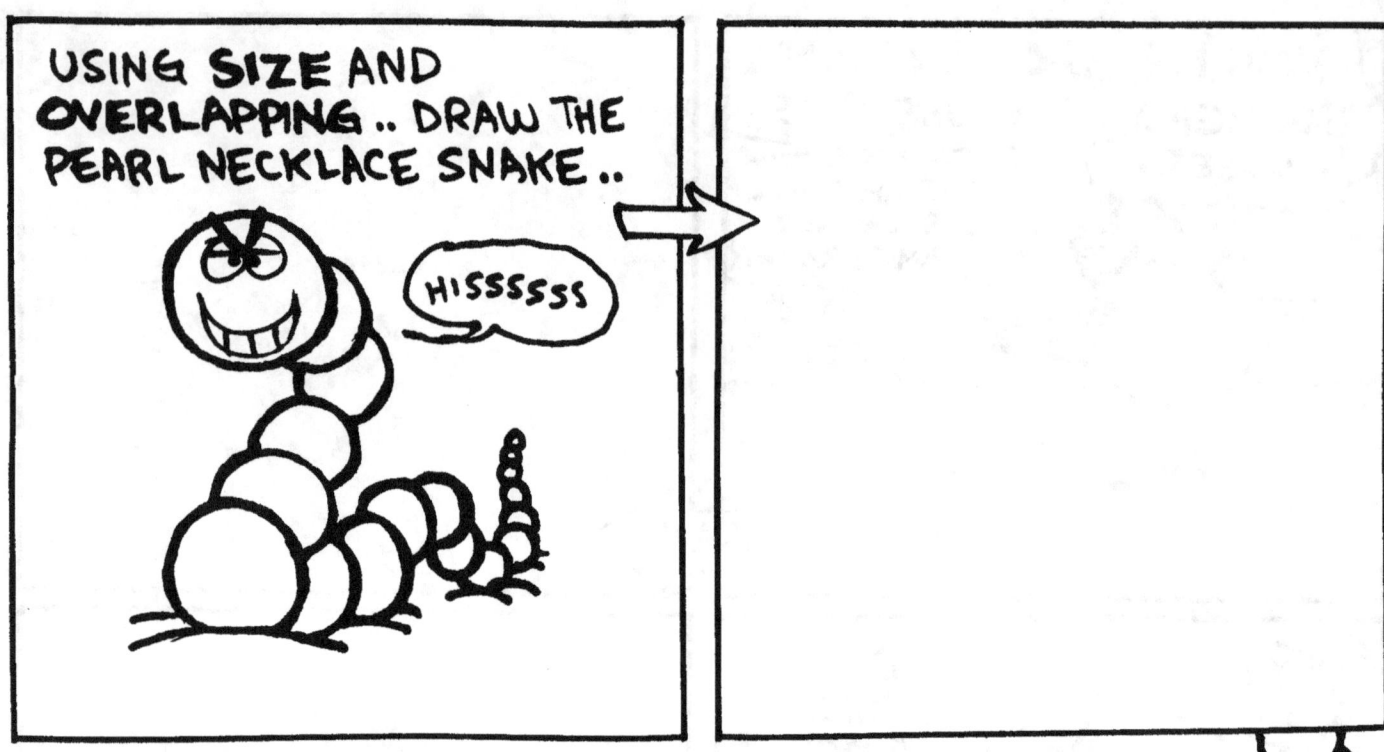

USING **SIZE** AND **OVERLAPPING** .. DRAW THE PEARL NECKLACE SNAKE ..

HISSSSSS

ON THE PEARL NECKLACE SNAKE .. NOTICE THE OVERLAPPING **GROUND LINES** .. PAY ATTENTION TO THE **BODY** SECTIONS OF THE SNAKE THAT BEND →

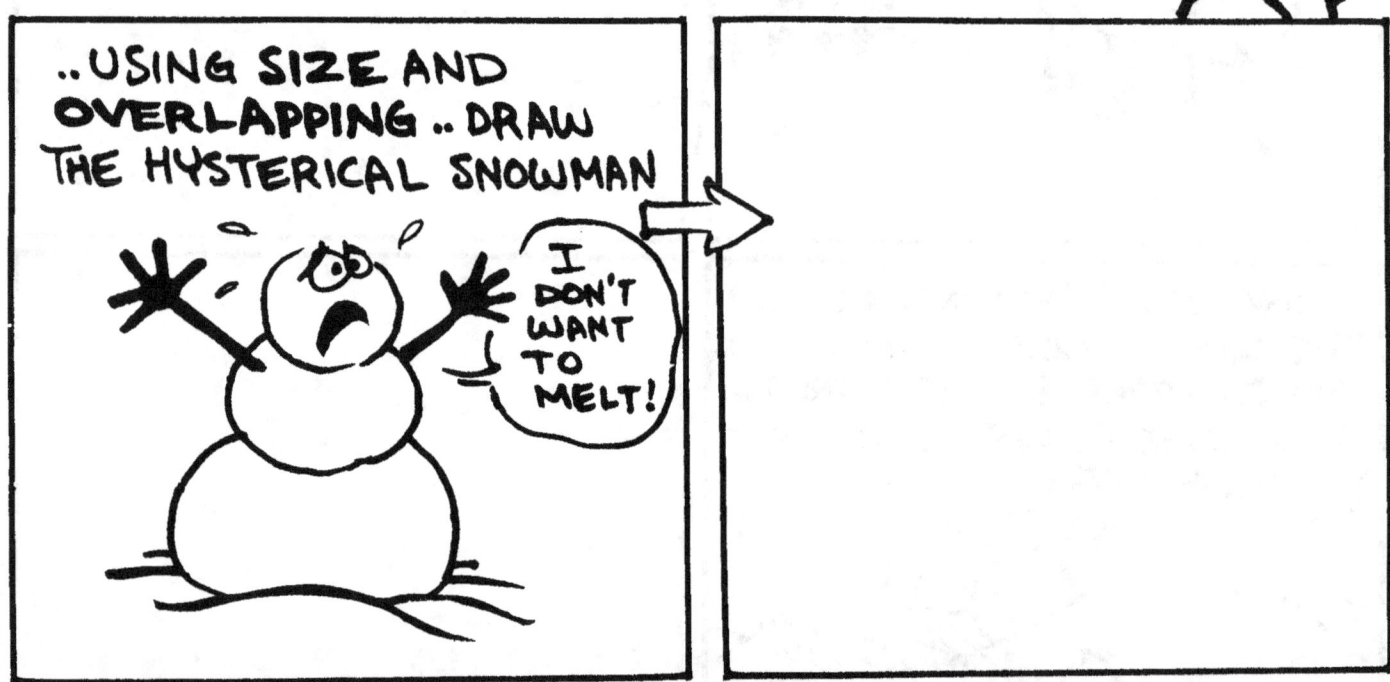

.. USING **SIZE** AND **OVERLAPPING** .. DRAW THE HYSTERICAL SNOWMAN

I DON'T WANT TO MELT!

PAY ATTENTION TO THE GROUND LINES .. AND THE **ARMS** OF THE SNOWMAN. THE NEAREST ARM IS LARGER .. AND **OVERLAPS** THE BODY ...

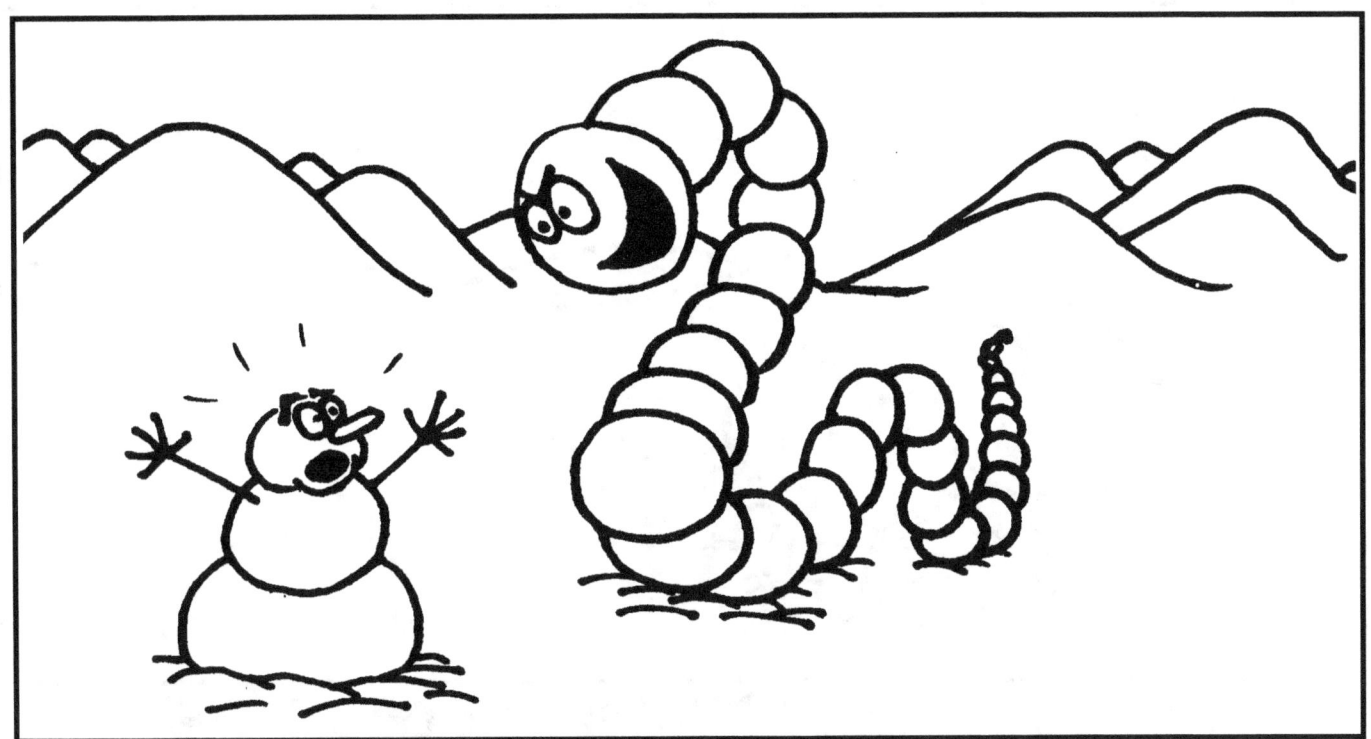

SIZE, OVERLAPPING WITH BACKGROUND..

NOW WE KNOW WHY THE SNOWMAN IS HYSTERICAL!
THE PEARL NECKLACE SNAKE IS GOING TO EAT HIM!
DRAW THEM BELOW.. AND PAY SPECIAL ATTENTION
TO THE OVERLAPPING HILLS IN THE BACKGROUND...

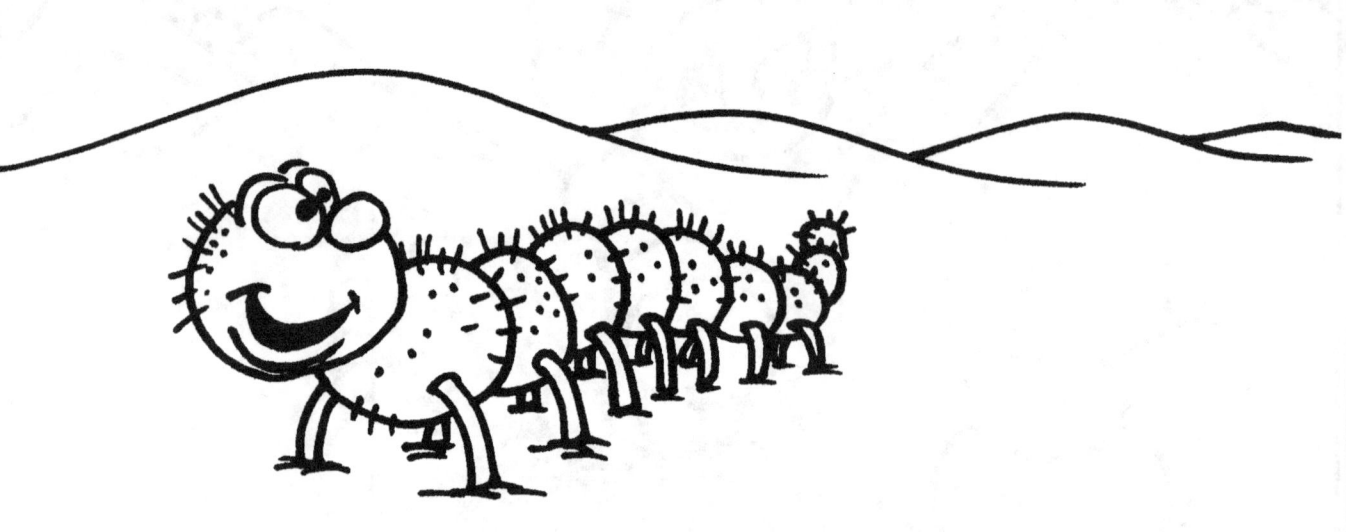

THE **LEGS** ON THIS CATERPILLAR OBEY THE PRINCIPLE OF **SIZE**.. THE LEGS CLOSEST TO US ARE **LARGER** AND **OVERLAP** HIS BODY. THE LEGS ON THE **FAR** SIDE OF HIS BODY **BARELY** SHOW.. AND DO **NOT** OVERLAP..!

DRAW! NOW!

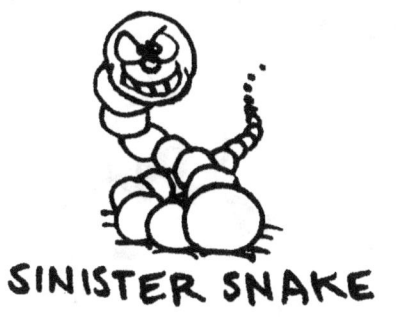

SINISTER SNAKE

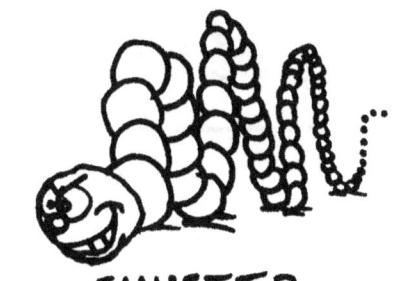

SINISTER SNEAKY SNAKE

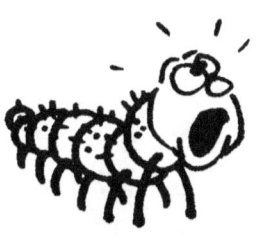

CATERPILLAR IN SHOCK

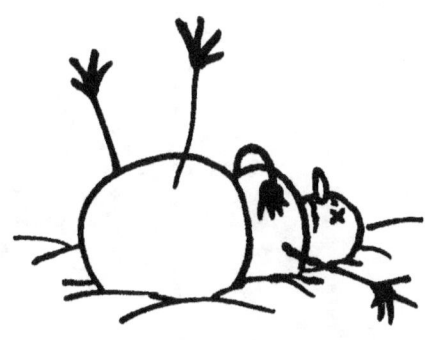

DEAD SNOWMAN

USE THE SPACE BELOW TO DRAW ONE OR MORE OF THE DRAWINGS IN THE COLUMN.

WRAPAROUND LINES

THIS IS THE THIRD PRINCIPLE OF PERSPECTIVE. WRAPAROUND LINES ARE ADDED TO A DRAWING TO BRING THE CURVED SURFACES INTO FOCUS.

THIS FELLOW LOOKS FLAT! HIS BELT DOESN'T WRAP AROUND HIM!

I'VE BEEN SQUASHED!

I LOOK GREAT! SIZE, OVERLAPPING.. AND A WRAPAROUND BELT LINE COMBINE.. AND I AM PLUMP!

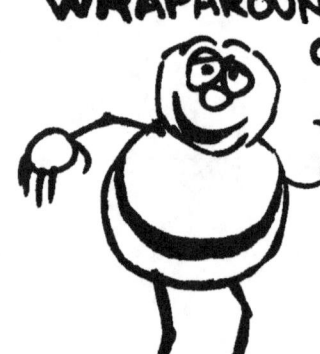

YOU TRY IT..

DRAW ME THIS WAY.. NOW MY BODY OVERLAPS MY HEAD.. AND MY WRAP-AROUND LINE POKES MY STOMACH FORWARD..

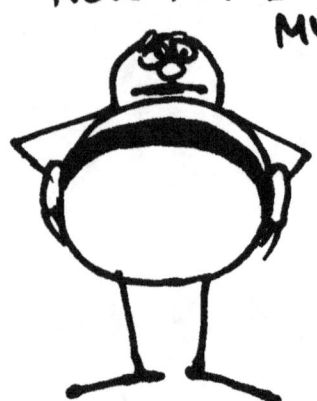

DRAW THIS STRIPED
EASTER EGG ..

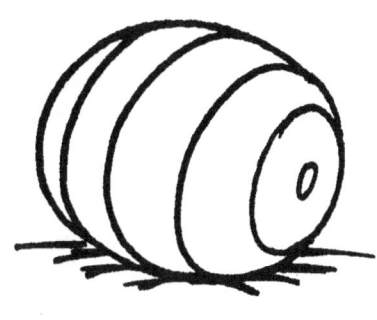

1. OVERLAPPING GROUND LINES UNDER THE EGG
   GIVE US THE ILLUSION THE EGG IS SITTING ON
   THE GROUND.

2. THE SHAFT ON THE TOP PASSES THROUGH THE TOP.
   WE OVERLAP THE TOP WITH THE SHAFT.
   THE BOTTOM POINT OF THE SHAFT IS BARELY
   VISIBLE AND IS NOT OVERLAPPED.

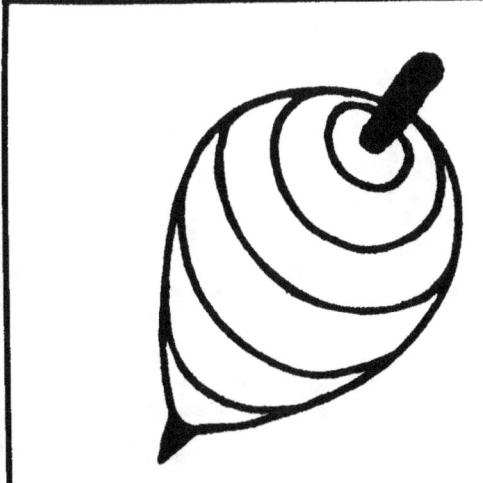

DRAW THIS TOP.

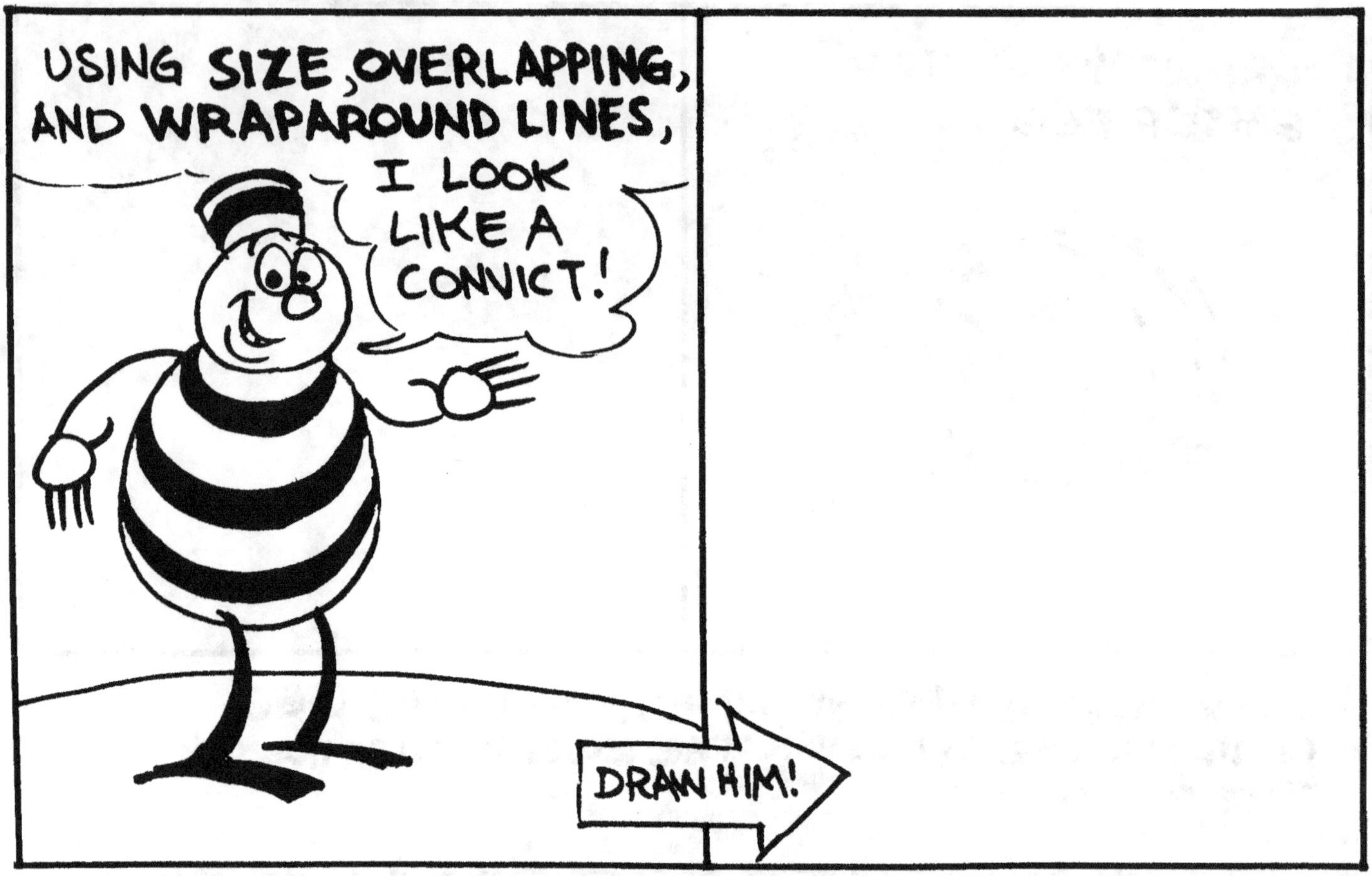
USING **SIZE**, **OVERLAPPING**, AND **WRAPAROUND LINES**,
I LOOK LIKE A CONVICT!
DRAW HIM!

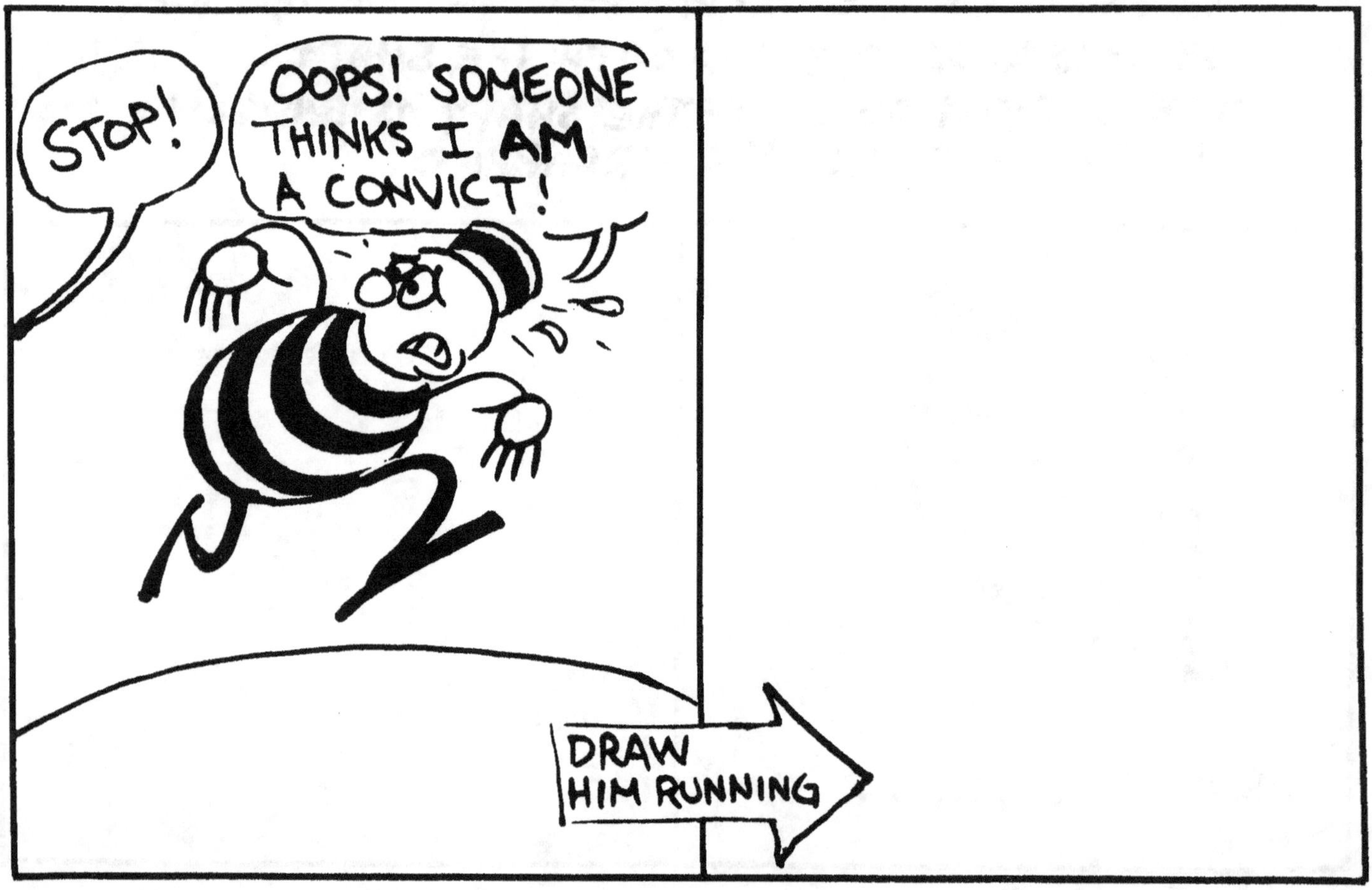
STOP!
OOPS! SOMEONE THINKS I **AM** A CONVICT!
DRAW HIM RUNNING

DRAW THIS BEE
SHAKING POLLEN OUT
OF THIS FLOWER..

THE PETALS OF THE FLOWER
CLOSE TO US ARE DRAWN
BIGGER. BE SURE TO WRAP
THE STRIPES AROUND OUR BEE.

THE ANT IS CONSTRUCTED
FROM OUR STRIPED
EASTER EGG AND TOP
SHAPES.

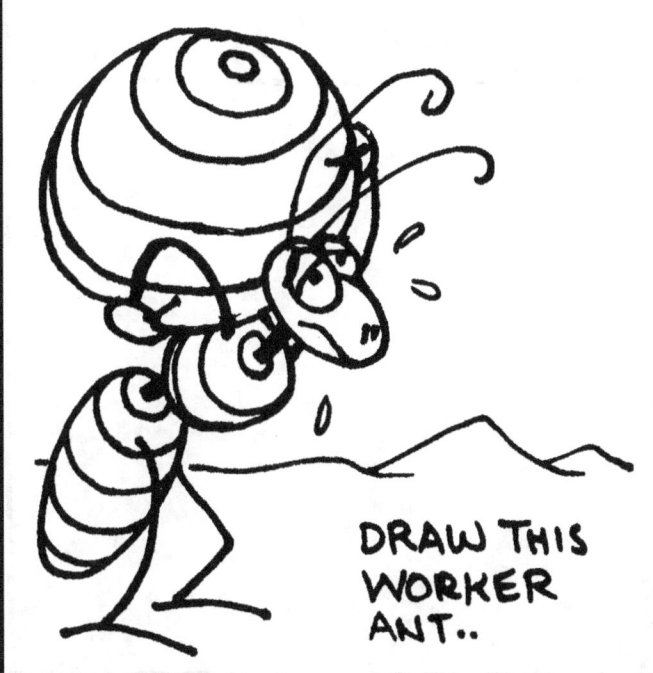

DRAW THIS
WORKER
ANT..

THE FOUR CORNERS OF THE CARTOON WORLD

THINK OF THE CARTOON PANEL AS A **WINDOW** INTO THE WORLD OF YOUR CARTOON PEOPLE.

IN THIS WORLD, YOU HAVE A **HORIZON**, A **FOREGROUND**, AND A **BACKGROUND**.

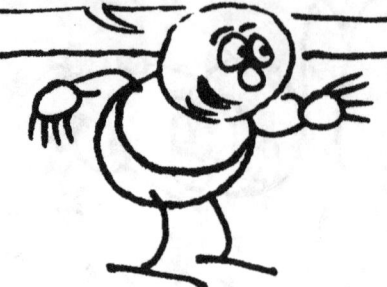

THE HORIZON LINE IS THE **DIVIDING LINE BETWEEN EARTH AND SKY** IN YOUR CARTOON WORLD!

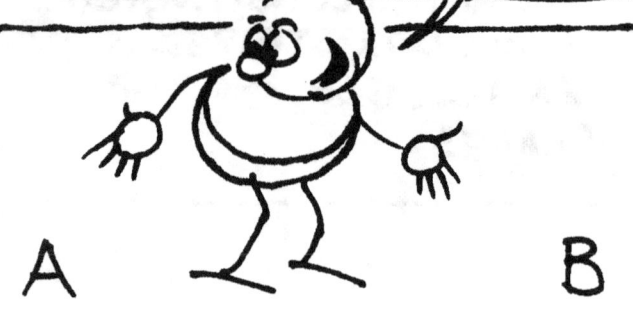

THE FOREGROUND.. WITH ITS **TWO CORNERS, A AND B**,.. IS IN FRONT OF ME.. EVERYTHING IS DRAWN LARGE IN THE FOREGROUND..

A   B

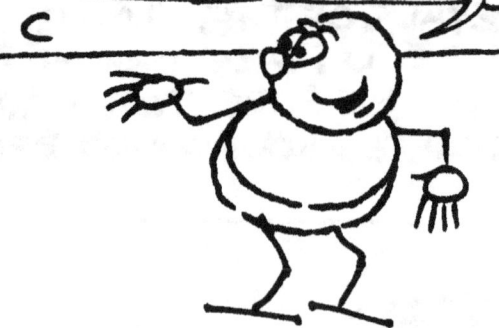

BEHIND ME IS THE BACKGROUND WITH ITS TWO CORNERS, C AND D... EVERYTHING IS DRAWN SMALL BACK THERE..

C   D

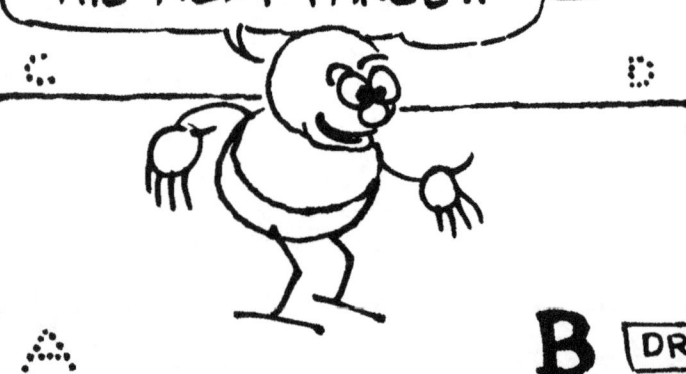

IN THIS PANEL I FACE FOREGROUND CORNER B... DRAW ME THIS WAY IN THE NEXT PANEL..

B ⟶ DRAW

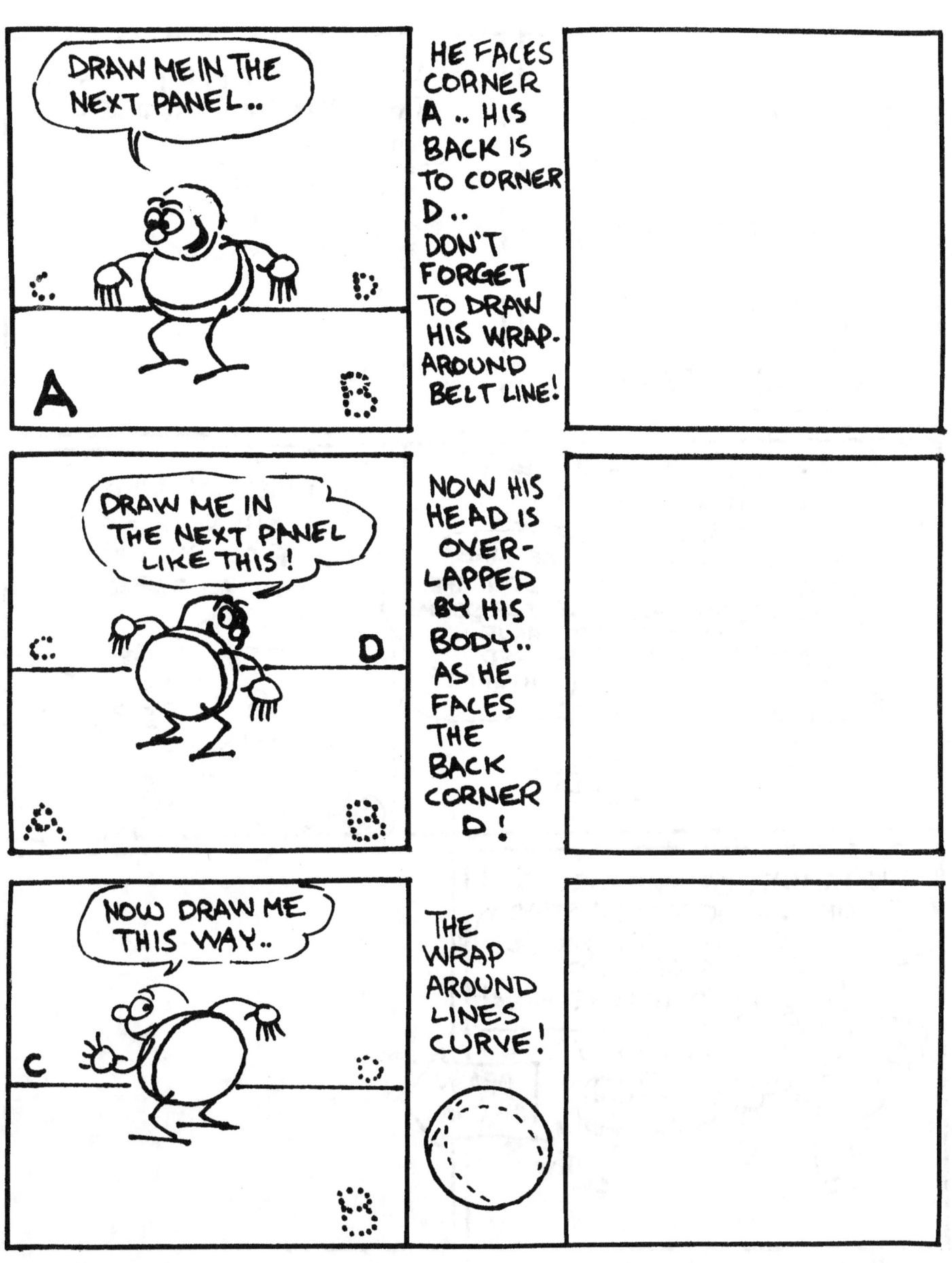

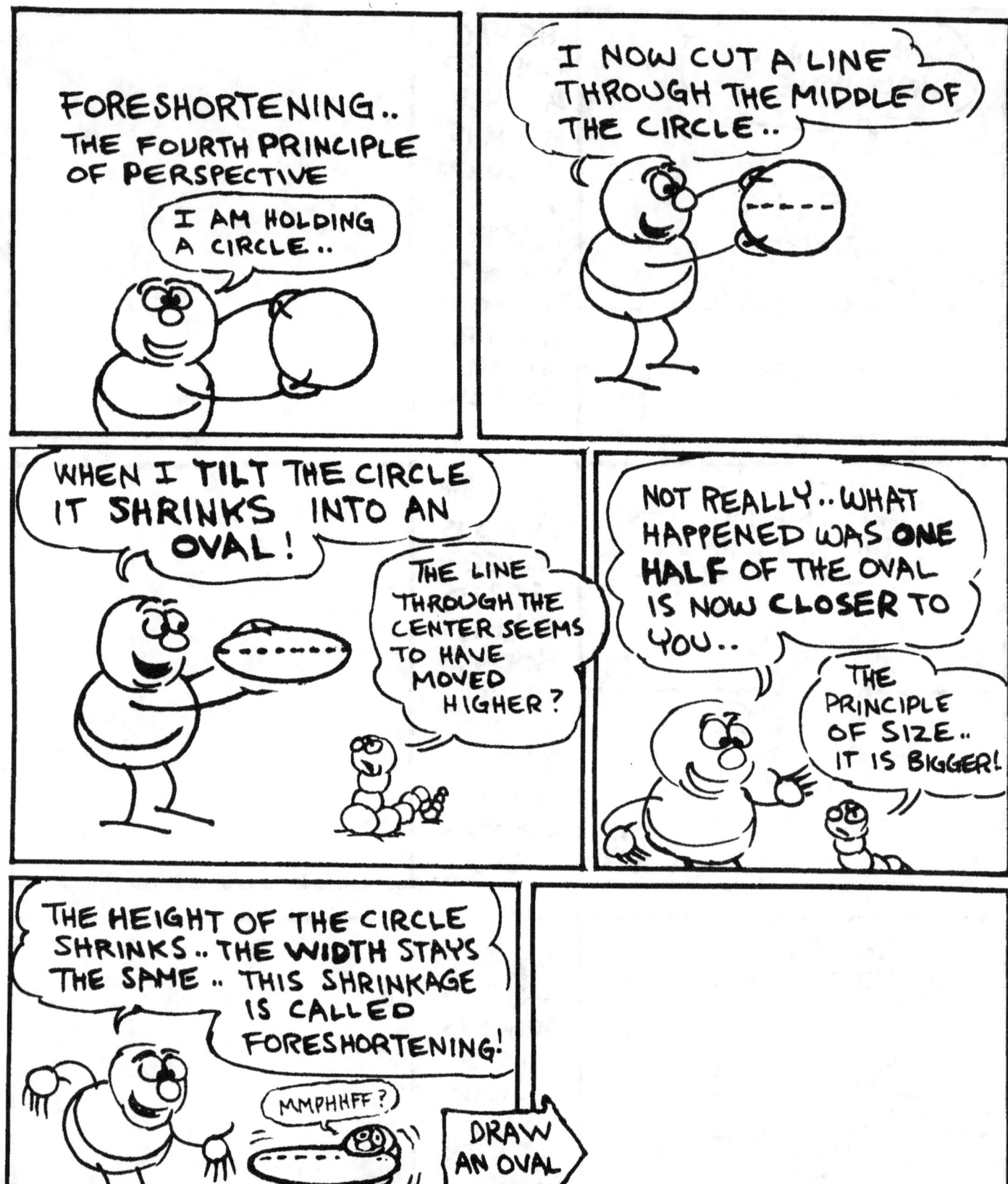

THREE STEPS TO A CYLINDER

1. DRAW AN OVAL ...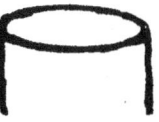

2. ADD TWO LINES OF EQUAL LENGTH ...

3. ADD THE BOTTOM LINE .. AND YOU HAVE A CYLINDER!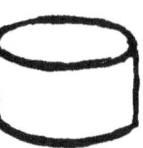

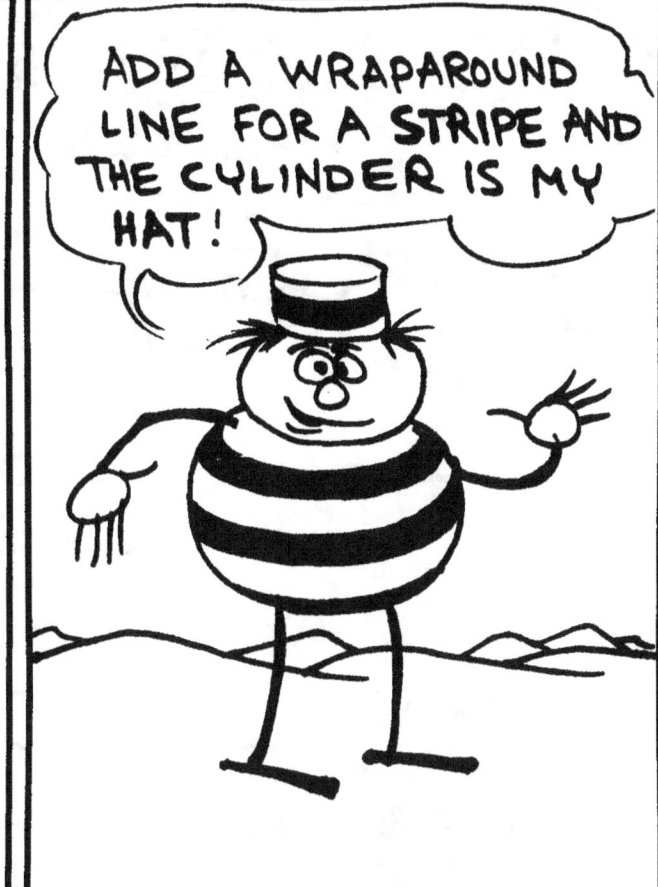

ADD A WRAPAROUND LINE FOR A **STRIPE** AND THE CYLINDER IS MY HAT!

THE MOST COMMON MISTAKES OF FORESHORTENING ...

1. 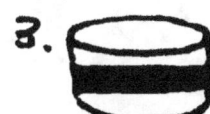 ← FLAT! PROFILE! NO PERSPECTIVE AT ALL!

2. ← SHOWS THE TOP OF THE HAT .. BUT IF WE SEE THE TOP FROM DIRECTLY ABOVE, WE COULD NOT SEE THE SIDE!

3. ← THE HAT IS RIGHT THE STRIPE IS WRONG!

4. 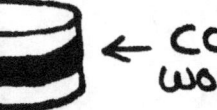 ← CORRECT! WONDERFUL!

NOW .. DRAW THE CONVICT AND HIS NEW HAT

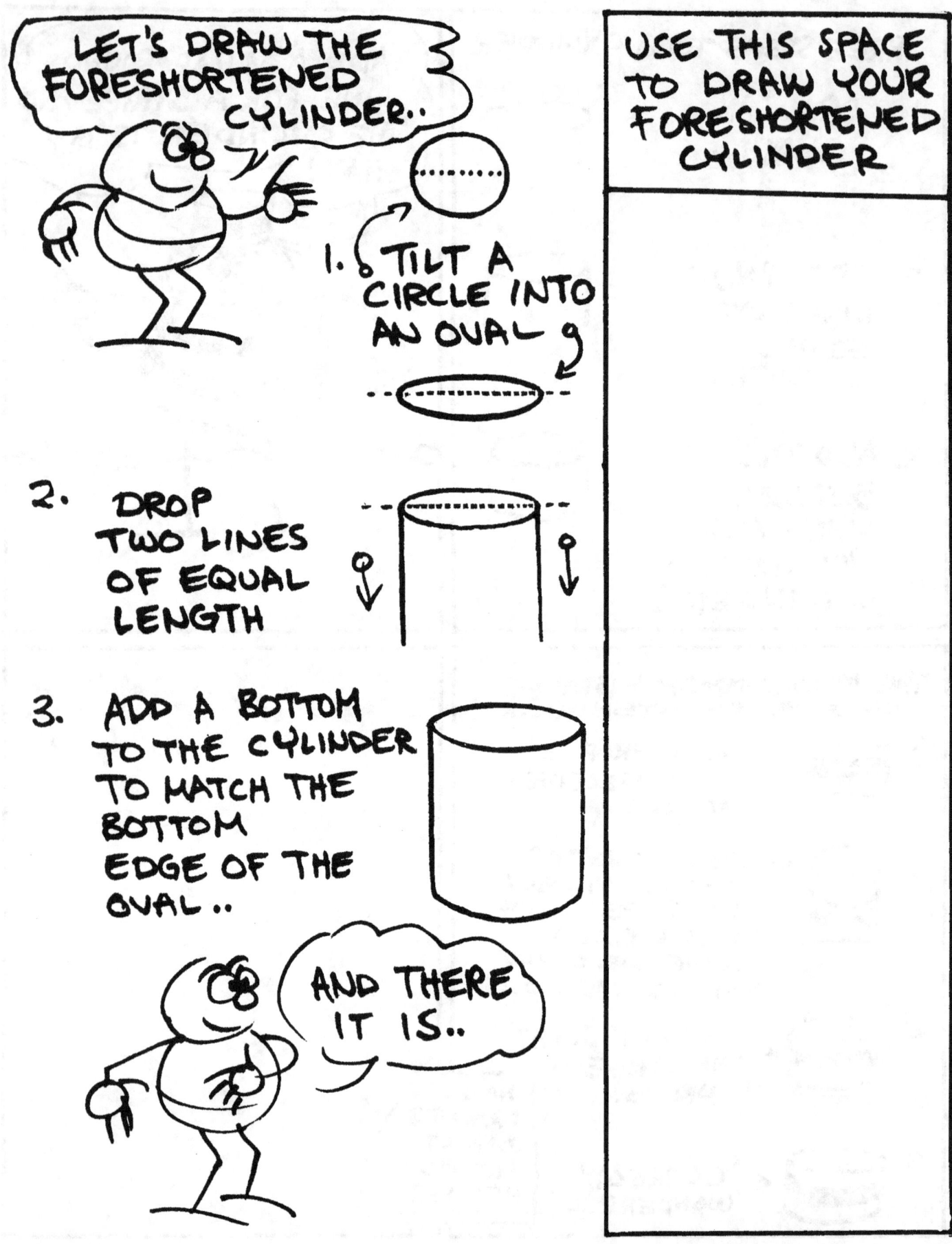

DRAW THE CYLINDER. INSIDE THE OVAL, DRAW A SMALLER OVAL. DRAW THIS SMALLER OVAL **CLOSE** TO THE **TOP** OF THE LARGER OVAL..

DRAW **WRAPAROUND** LINES ON THE **OUTSIDE** AND THE **INSIDE** OF THE CYLINDER..

— FRONT SIDE —

THE SMALLER OVAL BECOMES THE **INSIDE EDGE** OF A **HOLLOW** CYLINDER. ONE SIDE OF THIS CYLINDER.. THE FRONT SIDE IS **CLOSER** TO US.. SO IT IS BIGGER!

ADD VERTICAL LINES FOR BRICKS.. AND YOU HAVE A WELL.. DRAW THIS WELL IN THE NEXT PANEL..

WE DRAW THREE PARALLEL AND VERTICAL LINES. THESE LINES WILL BE THE CORNERS OF OUR FORESHORTENED BOX. THE TWO OUTSIDE LINES ARE OF EQUAL LENGTH. THESE WILL BE THE SIDE CORNERS.
THE MIDDLE LINE IS LONGER THAN THE OUTSIDE LINES, BUT DOES **NOT** EXTEND ABOVE THEM. THIS WILL BE THE **FRONT CORNER** OF THE BOX **CLOSEST TO US.**

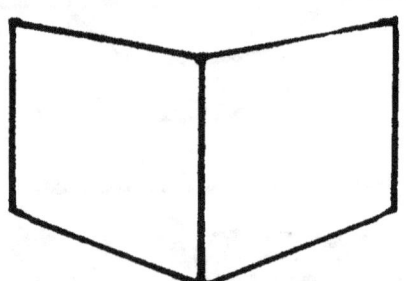

CONNECT ALL THREE LINES TO FORM THE **FRONT CORNER** AND TWO **SIDE CORNERS** OF OUR BOX!

THE **BACK CORNER** IS A **POINT** SLIGHTLY ABOVE THE LEVEL OF THE SIDE CORNERS. DO **NOT** EXTEND IT TOO **HIGH** OR IT WILL SPOIL THE ILLUSION. ALSO, DO **NOT PLACE** IT DIRECTLY ABOVE THE FRONT CORNER LINE.

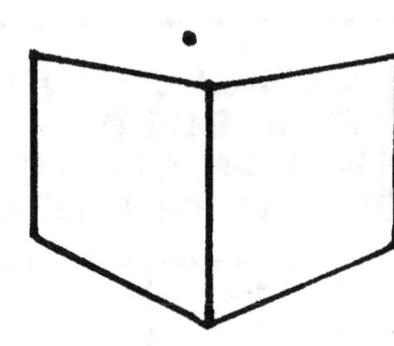

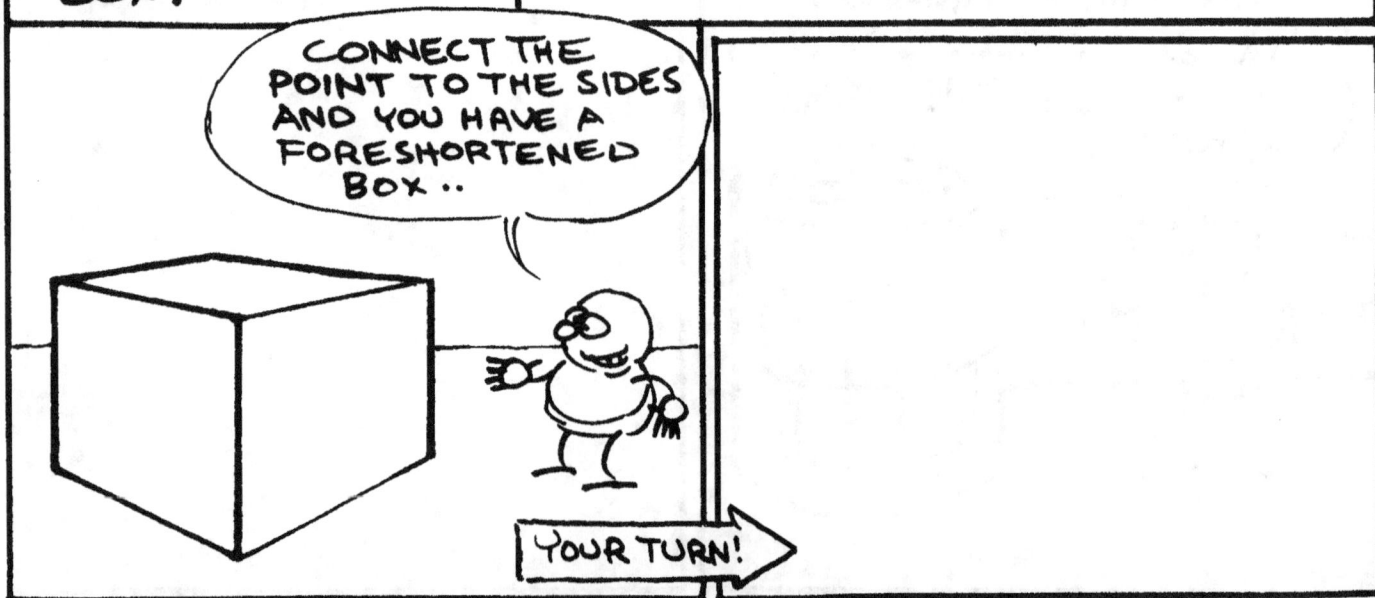

CONNECT THE POINT TO THE SIDES AND YOU HAVE A FORESHORTENED BOX..

YOUR TURN!

THE FORESHORTENED BOX...VIEWED FROM BELOW..!

IN THIS EXERCISE, THE FRONT CORNER LINE EXTENDS **ABOVE** THE SIDE LINES BUT NOT BELOW THEM.

1.

2.

3.

4.

YOUR TURN AGAIN →

THE FORESHORTENED BOX ..VIEWED FROM THE SIDE

EXTEND THE FRONT CORNER LINE SLIGHTLY ABOVE AND BELOW THE SIDE LINES..

1.

2.

JAIL

YOUR TURN →

THE FORESHORTENED BOX WITH THE INSIDE VISIBLE

←·········· ADD A BACK CORNER LINE..

YOUR TURN →

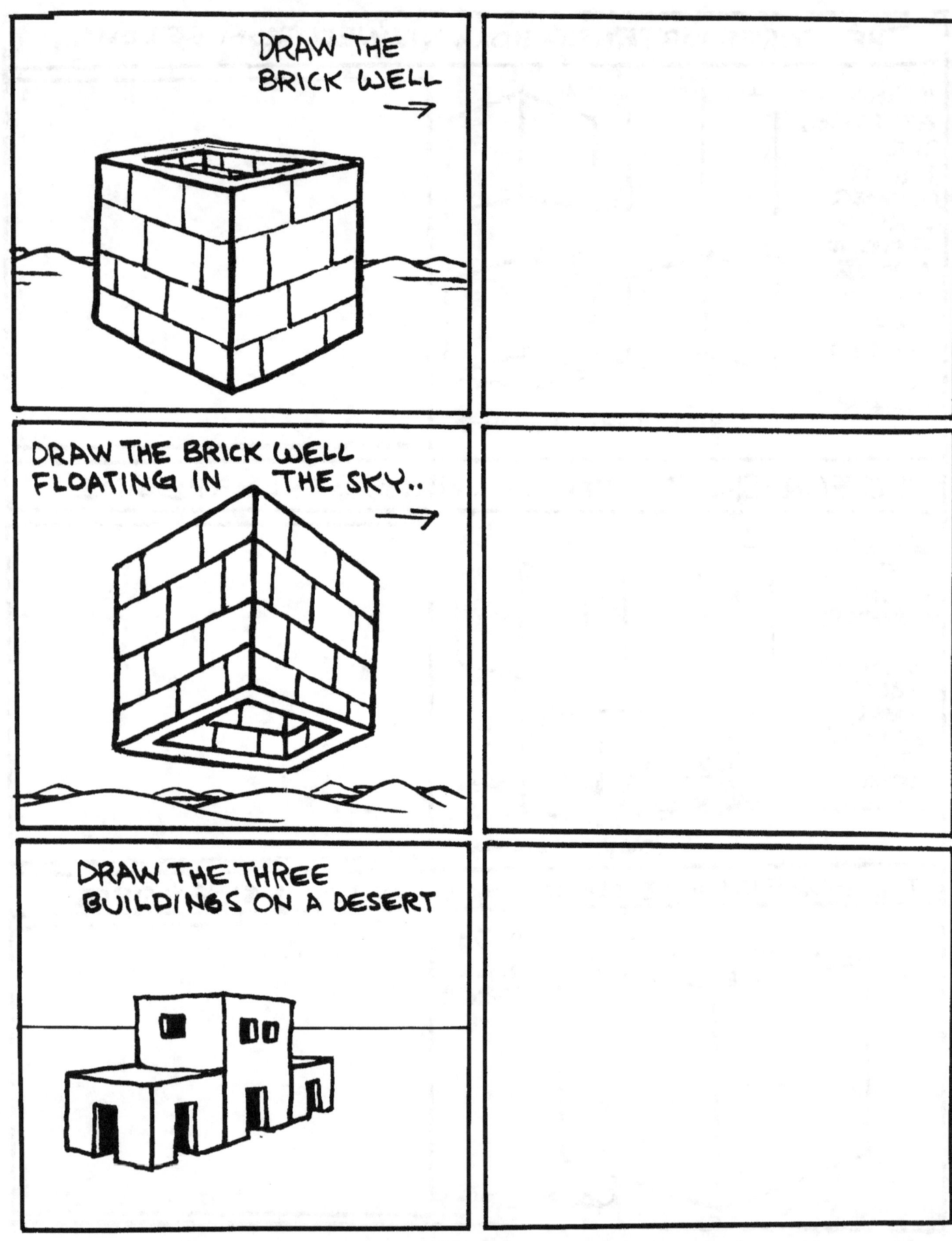

THE FORESHORTENED FENCE

1.

2.

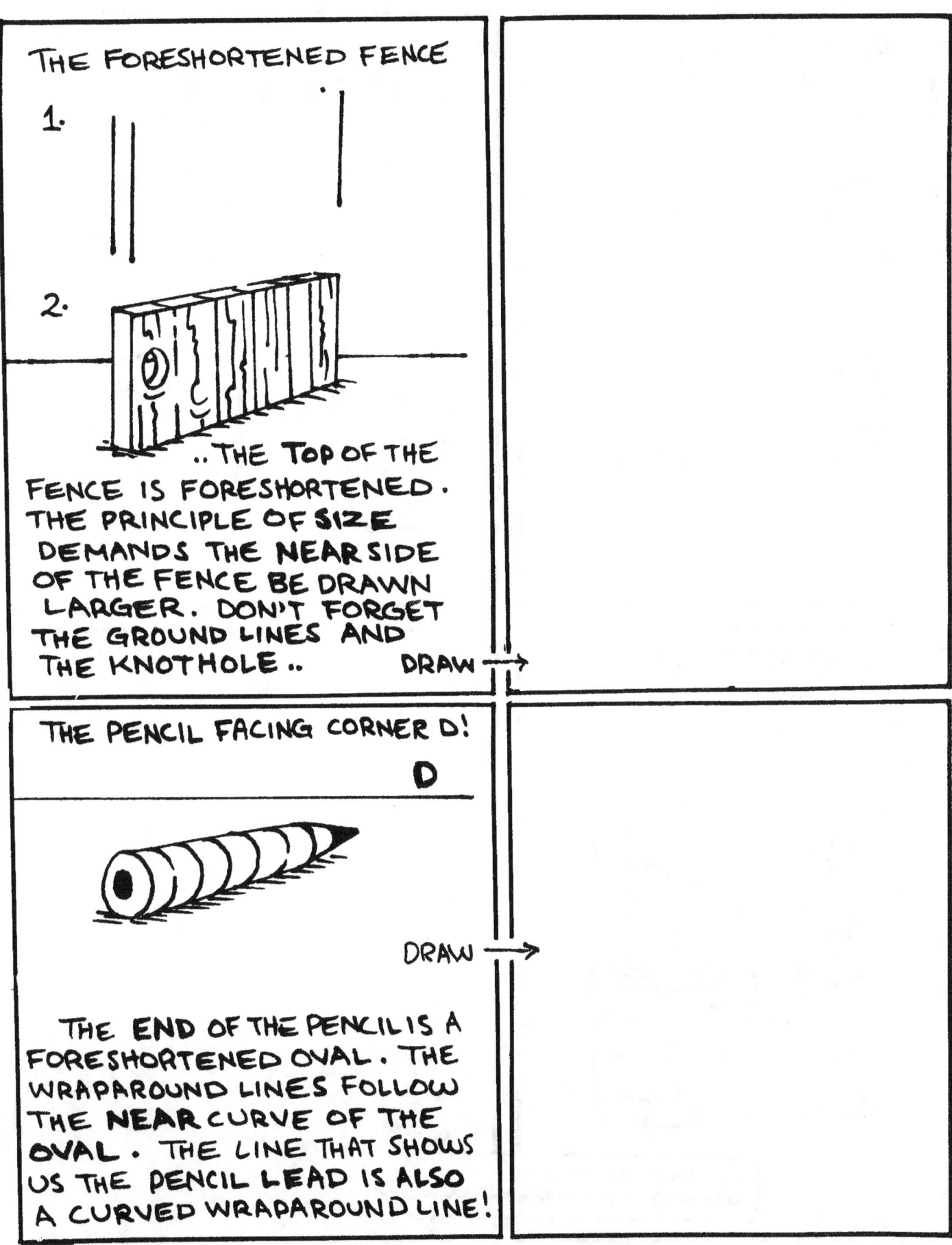

.. THE **TOP** OF THE FENCE IS FORESHORTENED. THE PRINCIPLE OF **SIZE** DEMANDS THE **NEAR SIDE** OF THE FENCE BE DRAWN LARGER. DON'T FORGET THE GROUND LINES AND THE KNOTHOLE ..   DRAW →

THE PENCIL FACING CORNER D!

D

DRAW →

THE **END** OF THE PENCIL IS A FORESHORTENED OVAL. THE WRAPAROUND LINES FOLLOW THE **NEAR** CURVE OF THE **OVAL**. THE LINE THAT SHOWS US THE PENCIL **LEAD** IS **ALSO** A CURVED WRAPAROUND LINE!

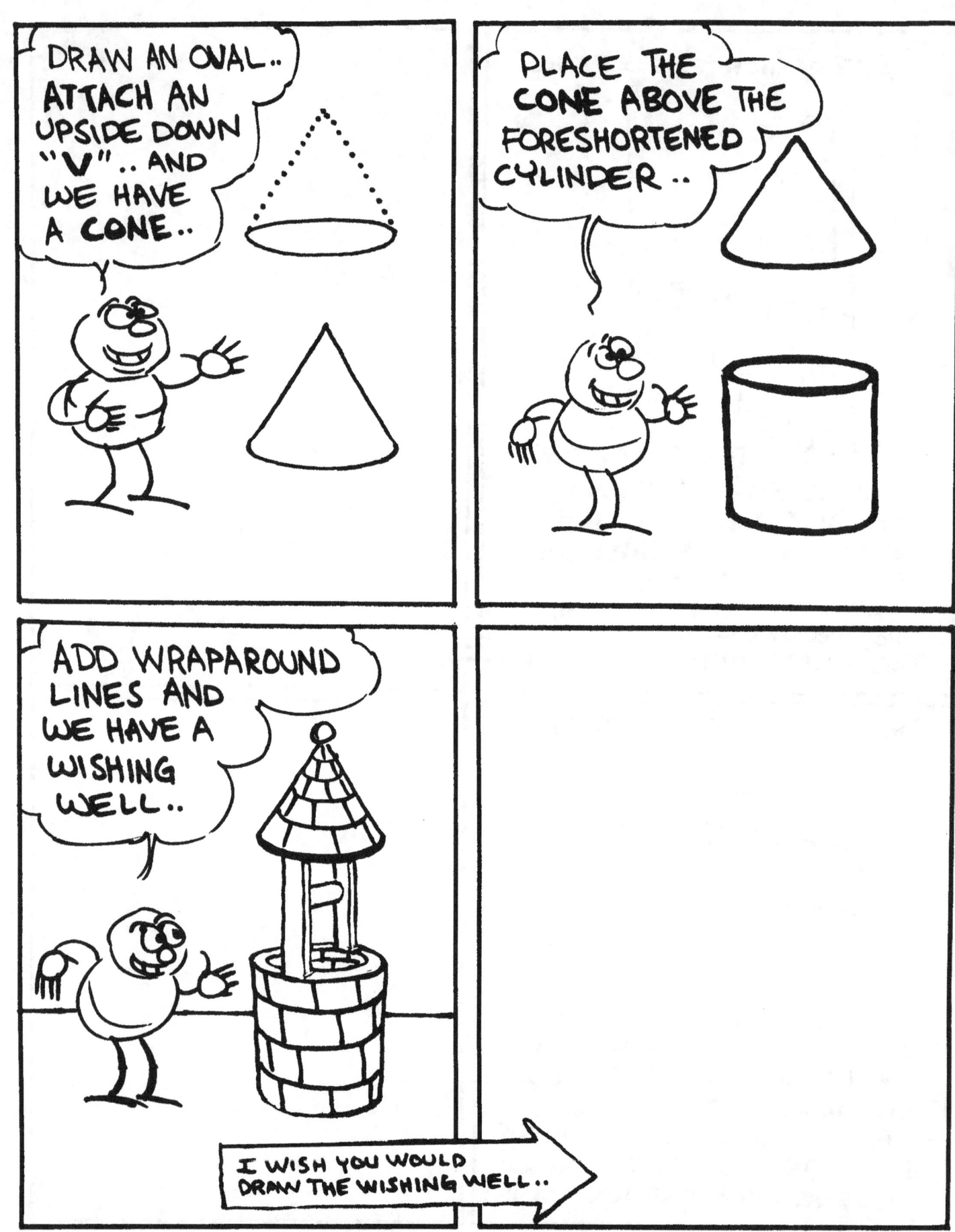

THE ESCAPED CONVICT

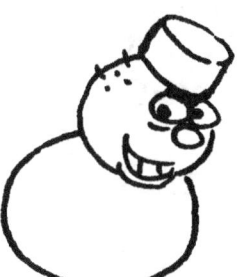

NOTICE MY HAT IS A TILTED FORESHORTENED CYLINDER

NOW I AM RUNNING .. THE PRINCIPLE OF **SIZE** SAYS MY LEG AND ARM CLOSE TO YOU ARE DRAWN BIGGER ..

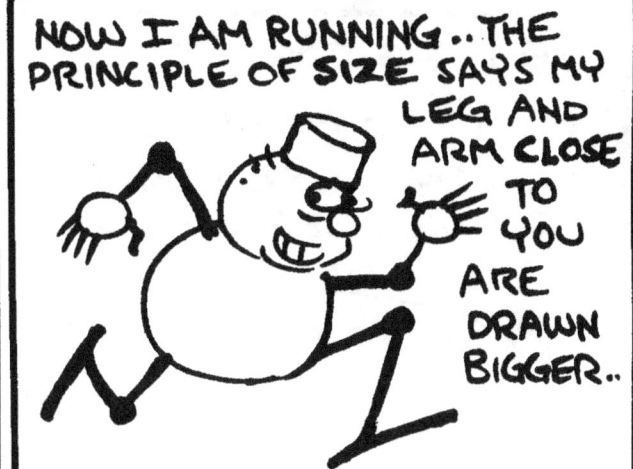

MY ARMS AND LEGS ARE CYLINDERS THAT MEET AT THE ELBOW AND KNEE ..

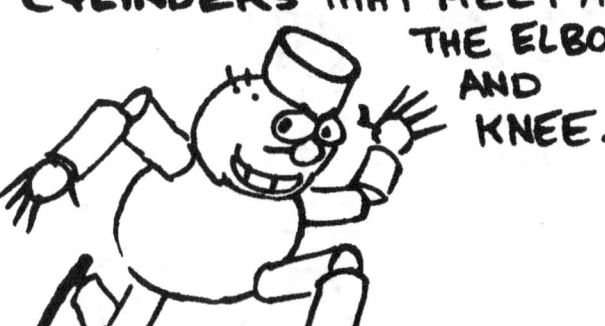

ROUND OFF THE KNEES AND THE ELBOWS ..

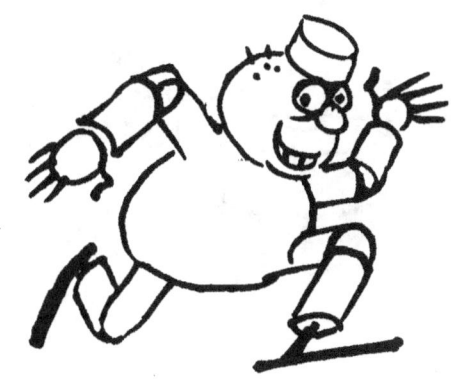

NOW WE ADD WRAPAROUND STRIPES ..

DRAW →

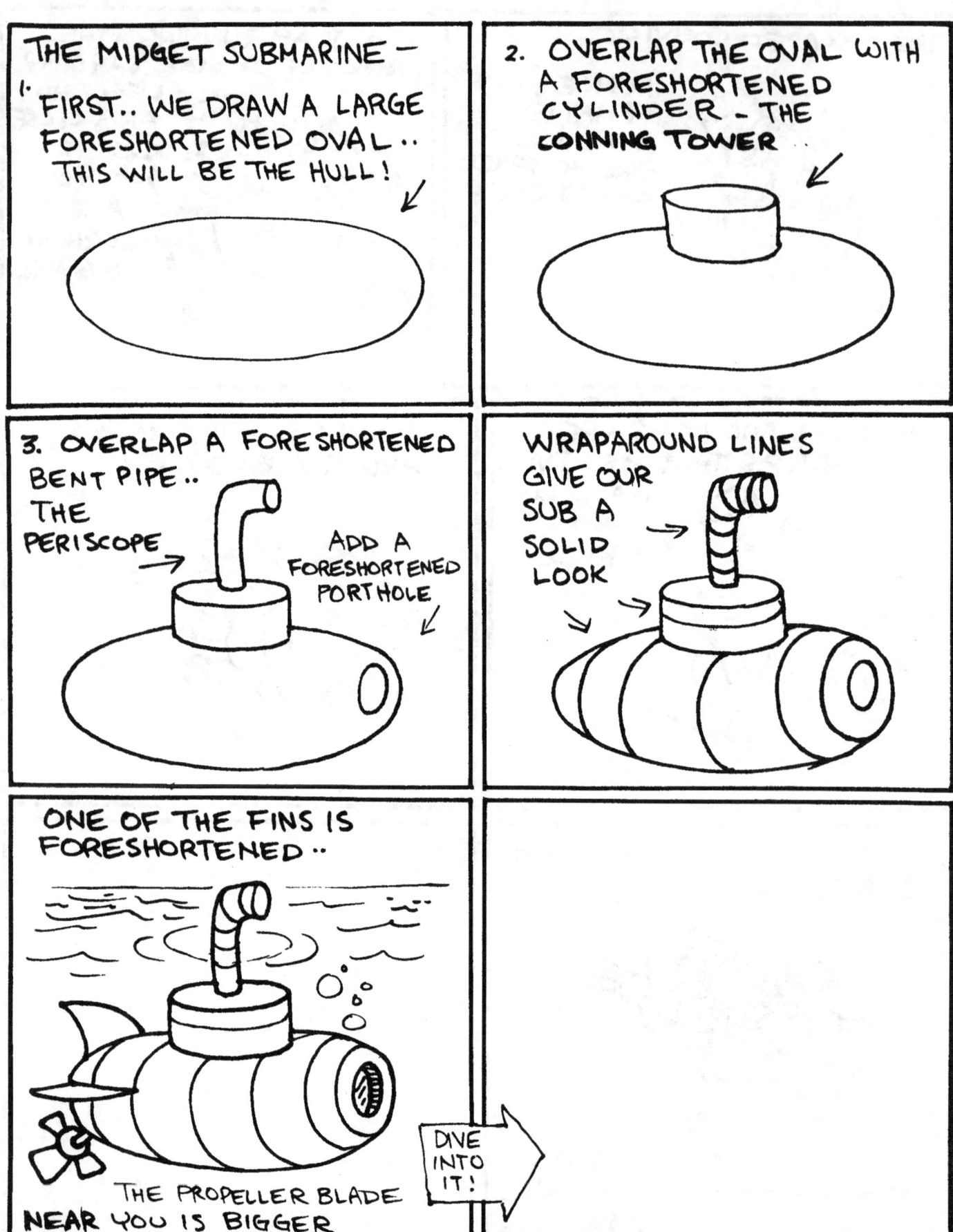

Panel 1: THE MIDGET SUBMARINE DIVING! THE OVAL IS FORESHORTENED TO THE EXTREME. IT LOOKS LIKE AN EGG!

Panel 2: THE SUB OVERLAPS THE CYLINDER THAT FORMS THE CONNING TOWER..

Panel 3: ADD THE FORESHORTENED OVAL PORTHOLE IN THE STERN .. AND THE PERISCOPE ..

Panel 4: WRAPAROUND LINES SHOW US HOW SOLID THE SUB IS .. AND THE DIRECTION IN WHICH THE PERISCOPE BENDS ..

Panel 5: THE SIDE FINS ARE FORESHORTENED.. THE PROPELLER BLADE CLOSE TO US ARE DRAWN LARGER..

THE MIDGET SUBMARINE
SURFACING —
WE DRAW THE SAME EGG SHAPED
FORESHORTENED OVAL.

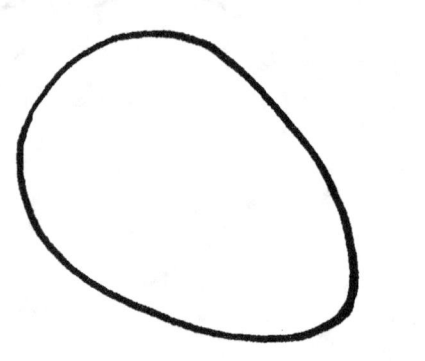

THE CYLINDER CONNING
TOWER IS THE SAME..

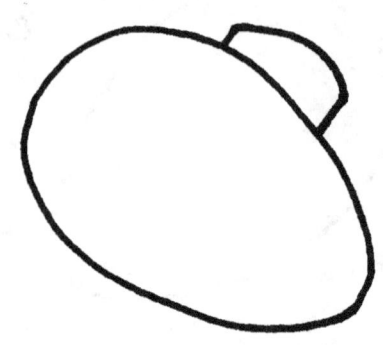

ADD THE PERISCOPE WITH ITS
OVAL LENS..
AND DRAW THE
FORESHORTENED
OVAL
BOW
PORT-
HOLE!

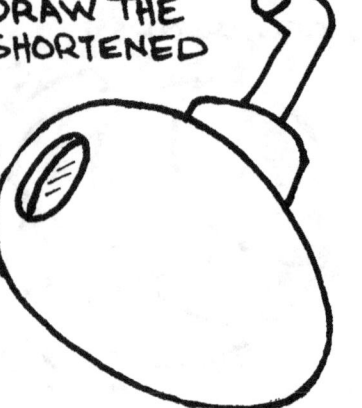

WRAPAROUND LINES
DIRECT THE BEND
OF THE PERISCOPE..
AND DEFINE THE
BULK OF
THE
SUB..

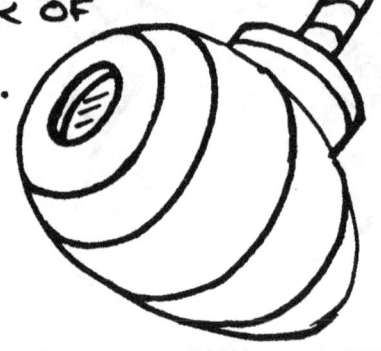

THE SIDEFIN FOLLOWS A
WRAPAROUND LINE OF RIVETS
THAT TRAVELS
ALONG THE SIDE
OF THE SUB..

THE FIN
IS ALSO
FORE-
SHORTENED.

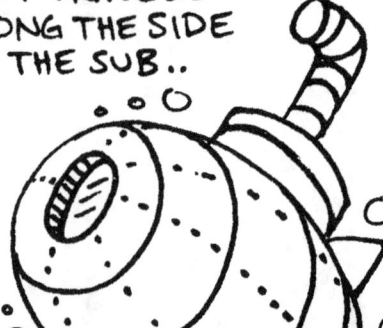

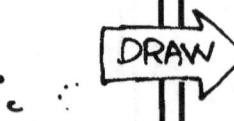
DRAW

DRAW THESE WEDGES OF CHEESE
PAY ATTENTION TO THE FRONT CORNER.
IT IS **NEARER** TO YOU .. THEREFORE LARGER!

1.   2.

1.   2.

1.   2.

1.   2.

1.   2.

1.   2.

1.   2.

1.   2.

THESE CHEESE SHAPES WILL HELP US DRAW FEET!

USING OUR PRINCIPLES OF PERSPECTIVE, WE WILL DRAW HANDS..

FIRST! **LOOK** AT YOUR HAND!

NOTICE CHEESE FEET

THE **PALM** IS A SQUARE SHAPE WITH **ROUNDED** CORNERS..

THE FINGERS ARE FORESHORTENED CYLINDERS.. OF DIFFERENT LENGTH! THEY **WRAP AROUND** THE THINGS WE PICK UP!

THE THUMB IS A CURVED CYLINDER EXTENDED FROM A PEAR-SHAPED BALL OF MUSCLE ON THE PALM!

AROUND THIS CONSTRUCTION WE DRAW SKIN.. AND ERASE ALL BUT A FEW WRAPAROUND LINES..

YOUR TURN!

THE
FINGERS
WRAP
AROUND
THE
CYLINDER..

THE BALL OF
MUSCLE
OVERLAPS
THE CYLINDER

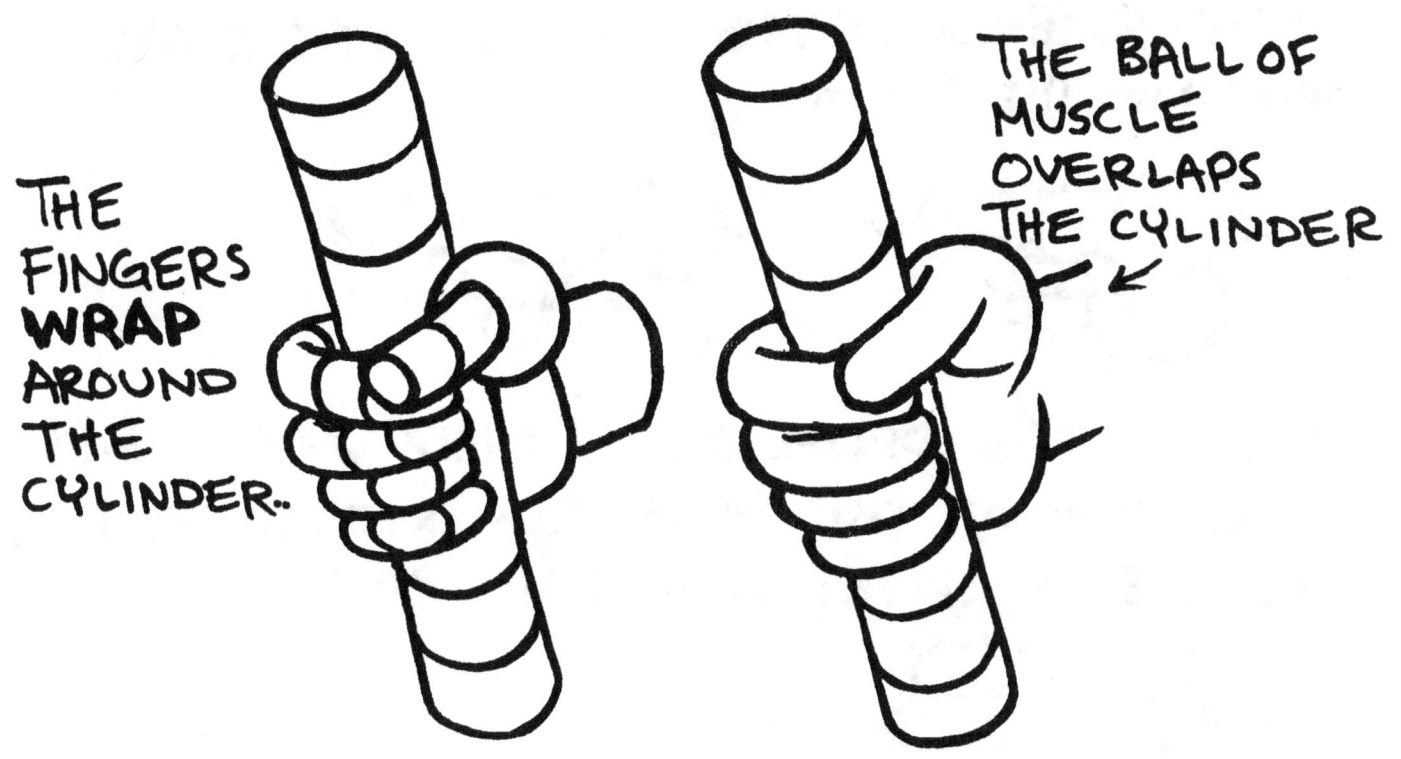

DRAW THE HAND HOLDING THE CYLINDER

USING **OVERLAPPING**..THE FINGERS CURL
AROUND THE PALM..

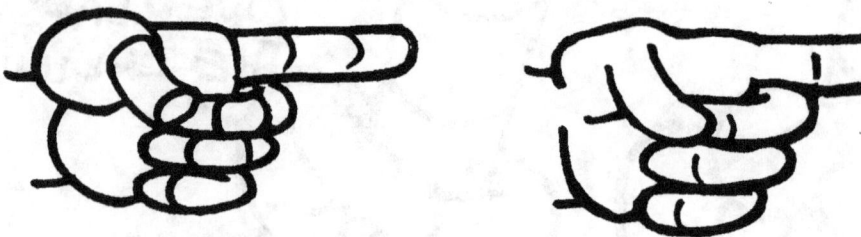

THE **THUMB** DROPS DOWN AND **OVERLAPS**
THE **TIPS** OF THE FINGERS.. NOTICE THE
THUMB IS **STILL** CURVED UPWARDS..

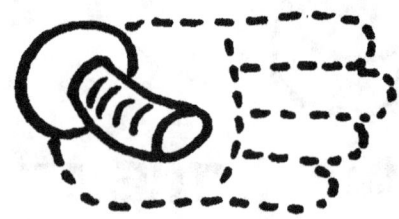

—————— **DRAW** THE HAND POINTING..—

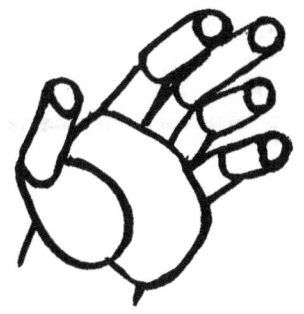 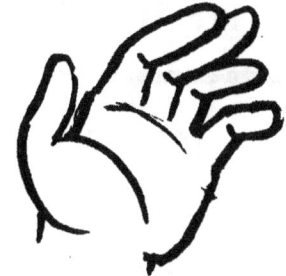 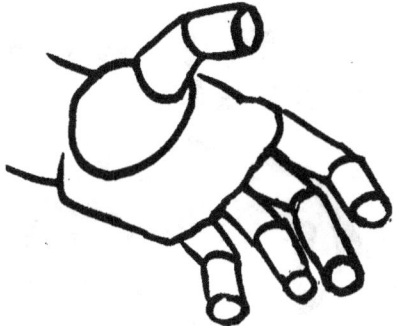

RELAX YOUR HAND..NOTICE
THE FINGERS TEND TO
CURL INWARD
TOWARDS YOUR PALM..

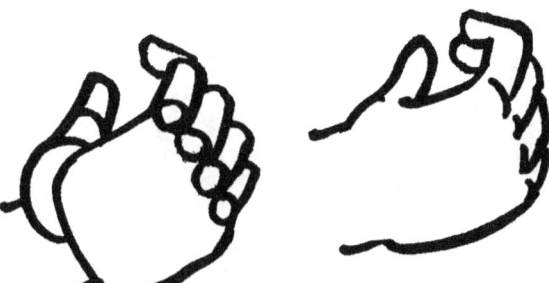 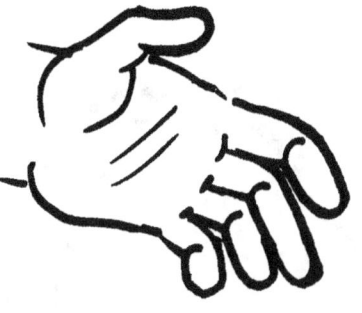

DRAW A FEW HANDS

THE FISTS — DRAW THEM ⭥

THE THUMB IS BEHIND THE FINGERS!

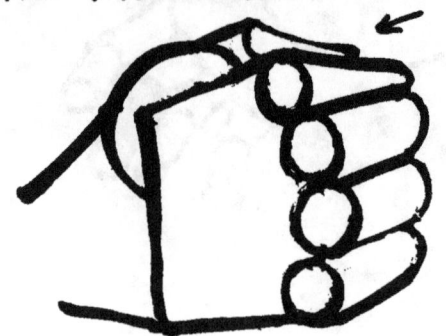

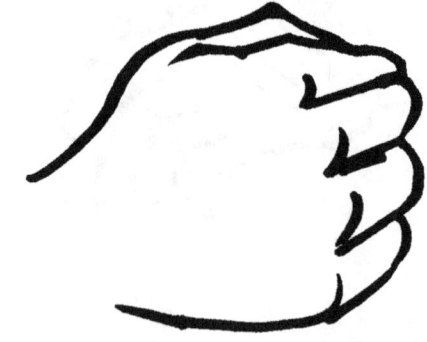

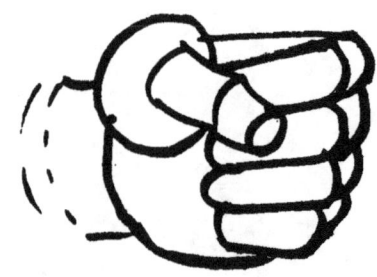

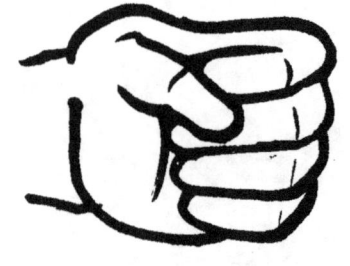

DRAW CYLINDER SAM
WITH HIS CHEESY FEET..

1.

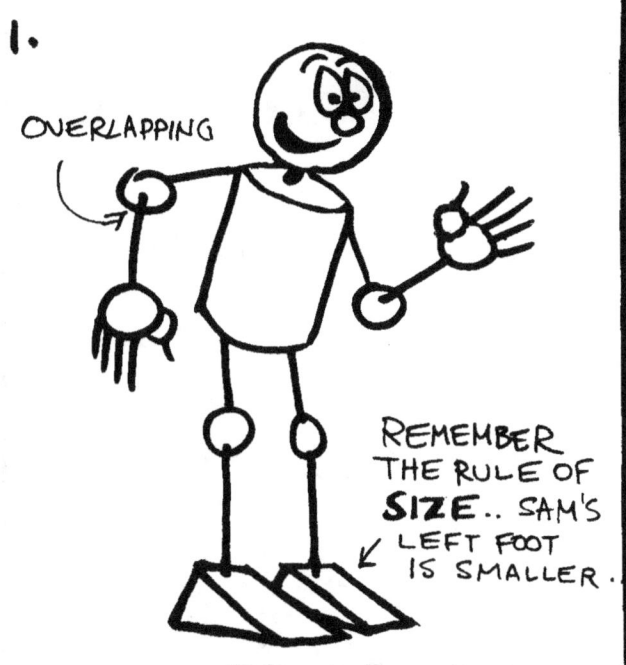

OVERLAPPING

REMEMBER
THE RULE OF
SIZE.. SAM'S
LEFT FOOT
IS SMALLER.

2. SAM WALKING

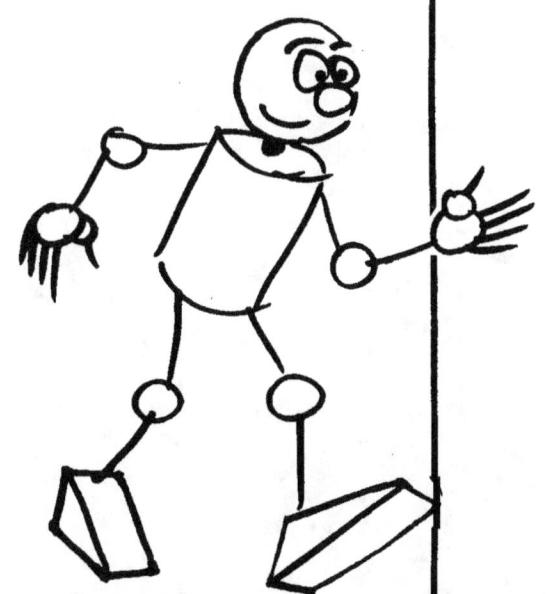

DRAW SAM IN THIS SPACE..

DRAW SAM WALKING ..

3.

SAM WALKING
TOWARDS YOU..

DRAW SAM ↓

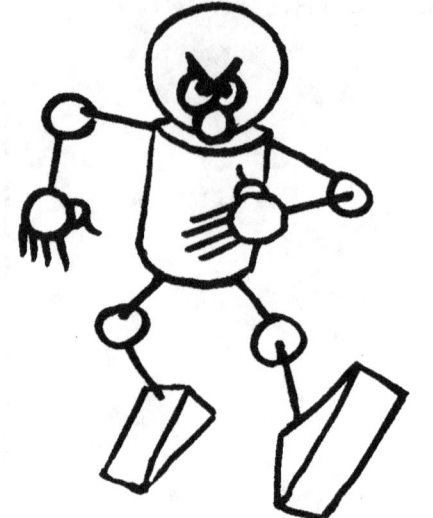

4.

SAM RUNNING ..

DRAW SAM ↓

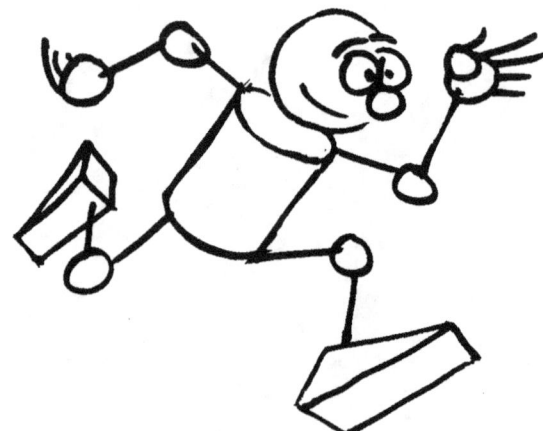

SHADING — THE 5TH PRINCIPLE OF PERSPECTIVE!

THE USE OF TWO SHADOWS INCREASES THE ILLUSION OF THREE DIMENSIONS IN OUR DRAWING..

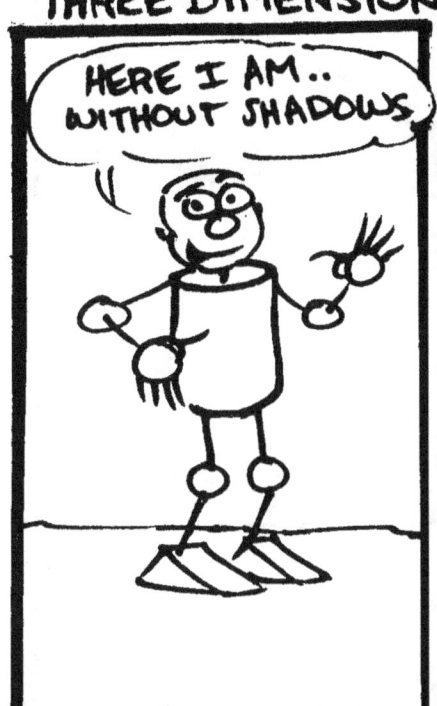

HERE I AM.. WITHOUT SHADOWS

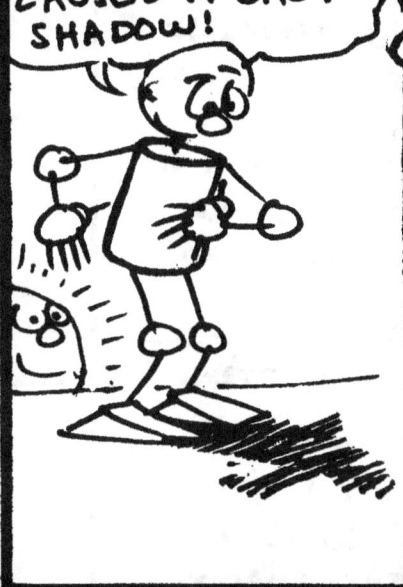

A SOURCE OF LIGHT BEHIND ME CAUSES A CAST SHADOW!

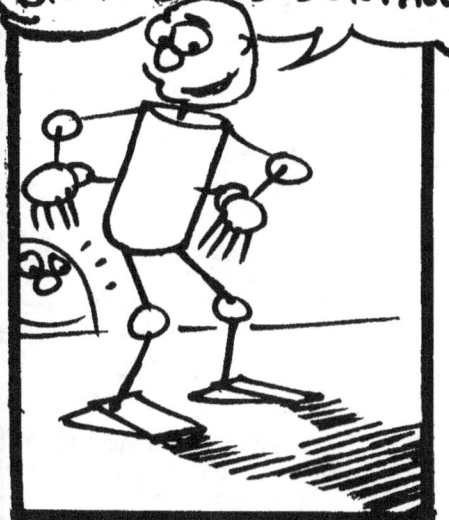

THIS CAST SHADOW LINKS ME WITH THE GROUND! I AM STANDING ON A SOLID SURFACE!

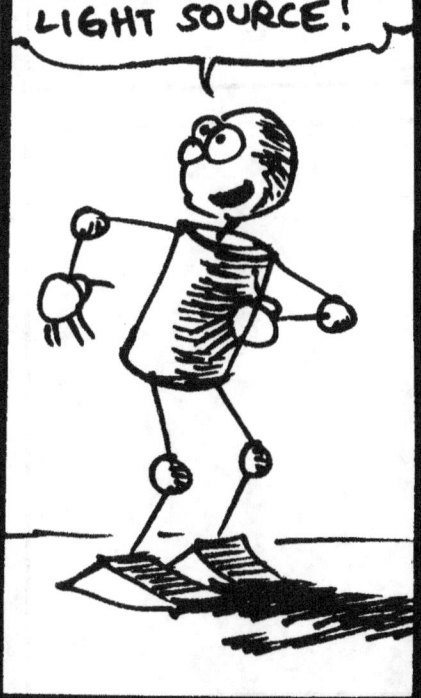

..THE SECONDARY SHADOW OCCURS ON ALL PARTS OF ME **OPPOSITE** THE LIGHT SOURCE!

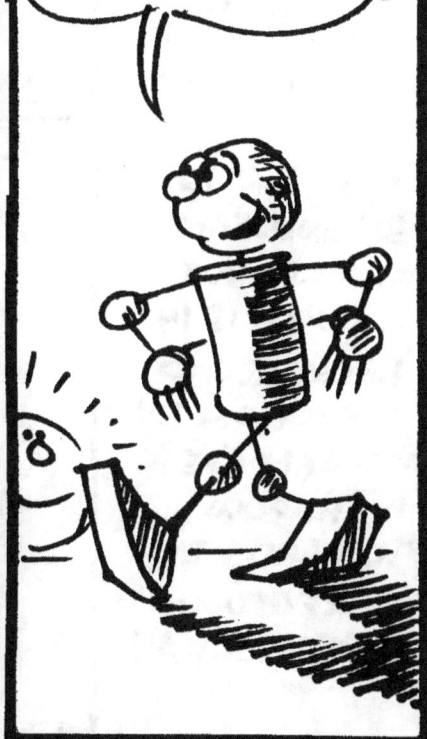

..THIS SECONDARY SHADOW GIVES ME SOLID WEIGHT—

ON THE NEXT TWO PAGES DRAW SAM AND HIS CAST SHADOW AND THE EXERCISES WITH THE SECONDARY SHADOWS! NOTICE ON SAM'S CYLINDER BODY THE SECONDARY SHADOWS ARE **WRAPAROUND** LINES INTERRUPTED BY LIGHT!

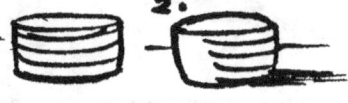

1.   2.

THE CAST SHADOW — AND CYLINDER SAM —
DRAW SAM AND HIS CAST SHADOW IN THE BLANK PANELS!

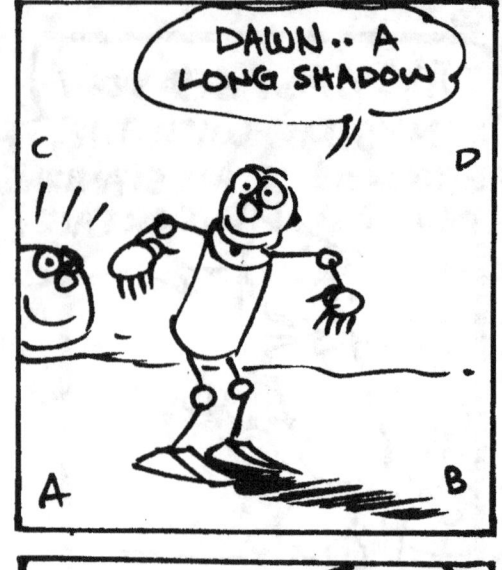

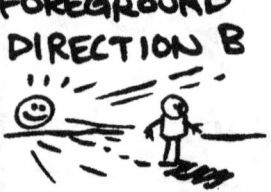

THE LIGHT IS BEHIND SAM.. COMING FROM THE BACKGROUND DIRECTION C.. THE SHADOW STRETCHES INTO FOREGROUND DIRECTION B

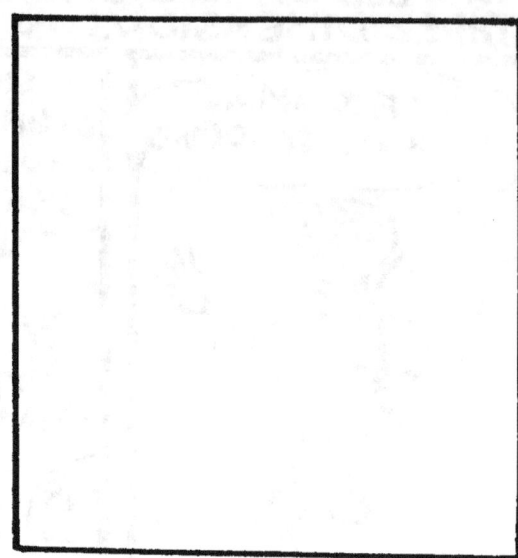

THE LIGHT IS NOW DIRECTLY ABOVE SAM! THE SHADOW IS SHORT..

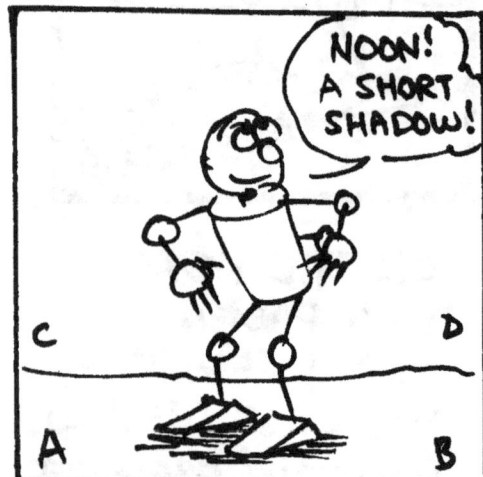

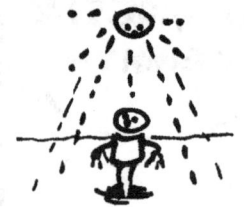

THE SUN IS BEHIND SAM AGAIN.. BUT NOW IT IS IN BACKGROUND DIRECTION D! SO SAM CASTS A SHADOW TOWARDS THE FOREGROUND DIRECTION A!

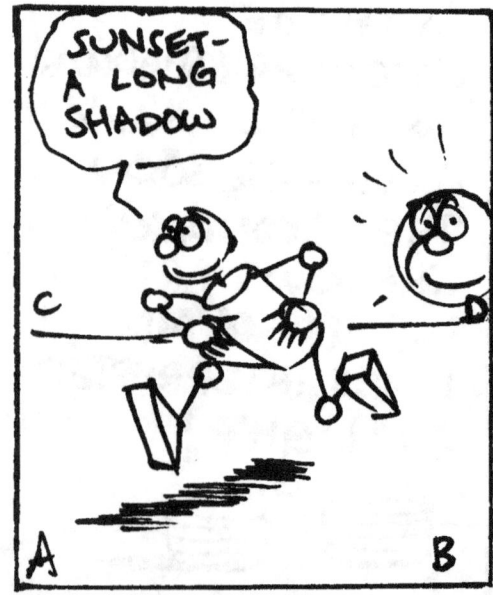

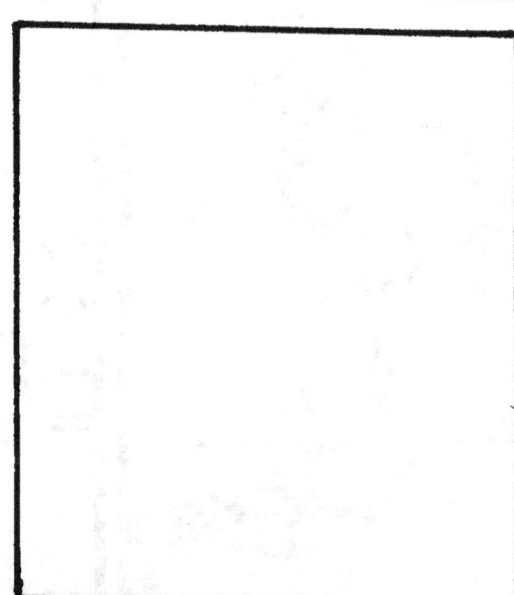

A BALL, A CUP, HOUSE AND A FEW ROCKS —
ADD CAST SHADOW AND SECONDARY SHADOWS
TO THESE OBJECTS AFTER YOU DRAW THEM
IN THE BLANK PANELS —

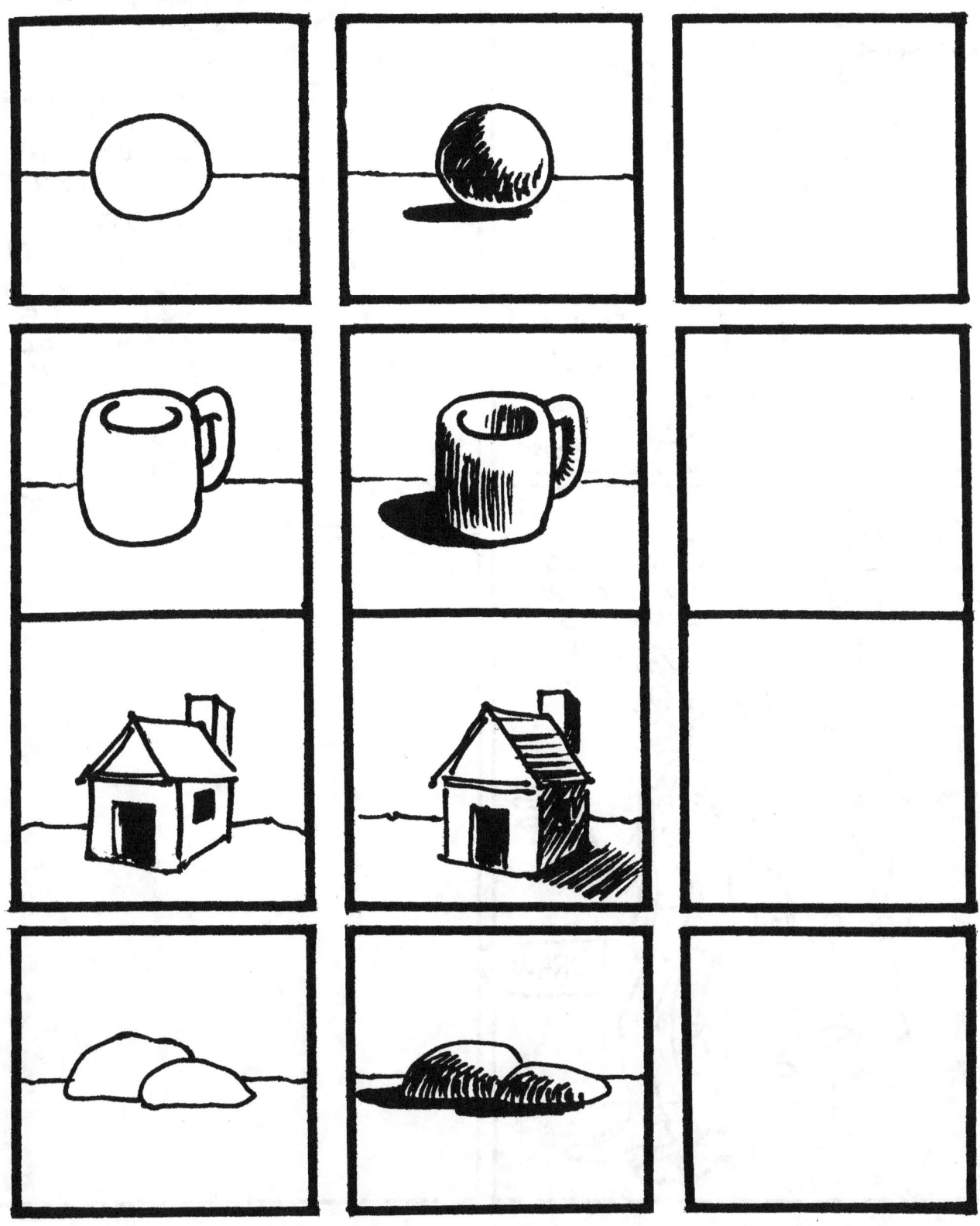

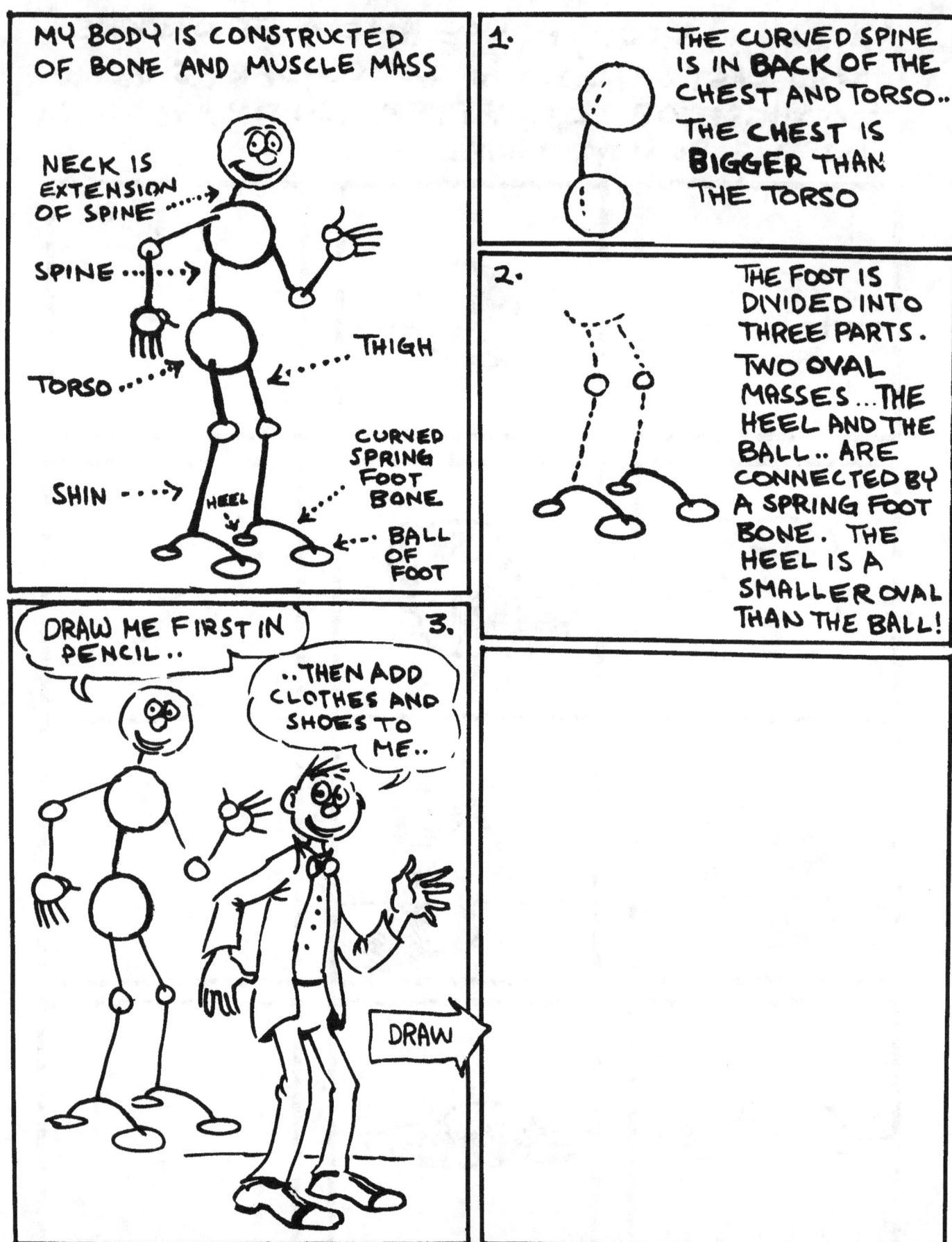

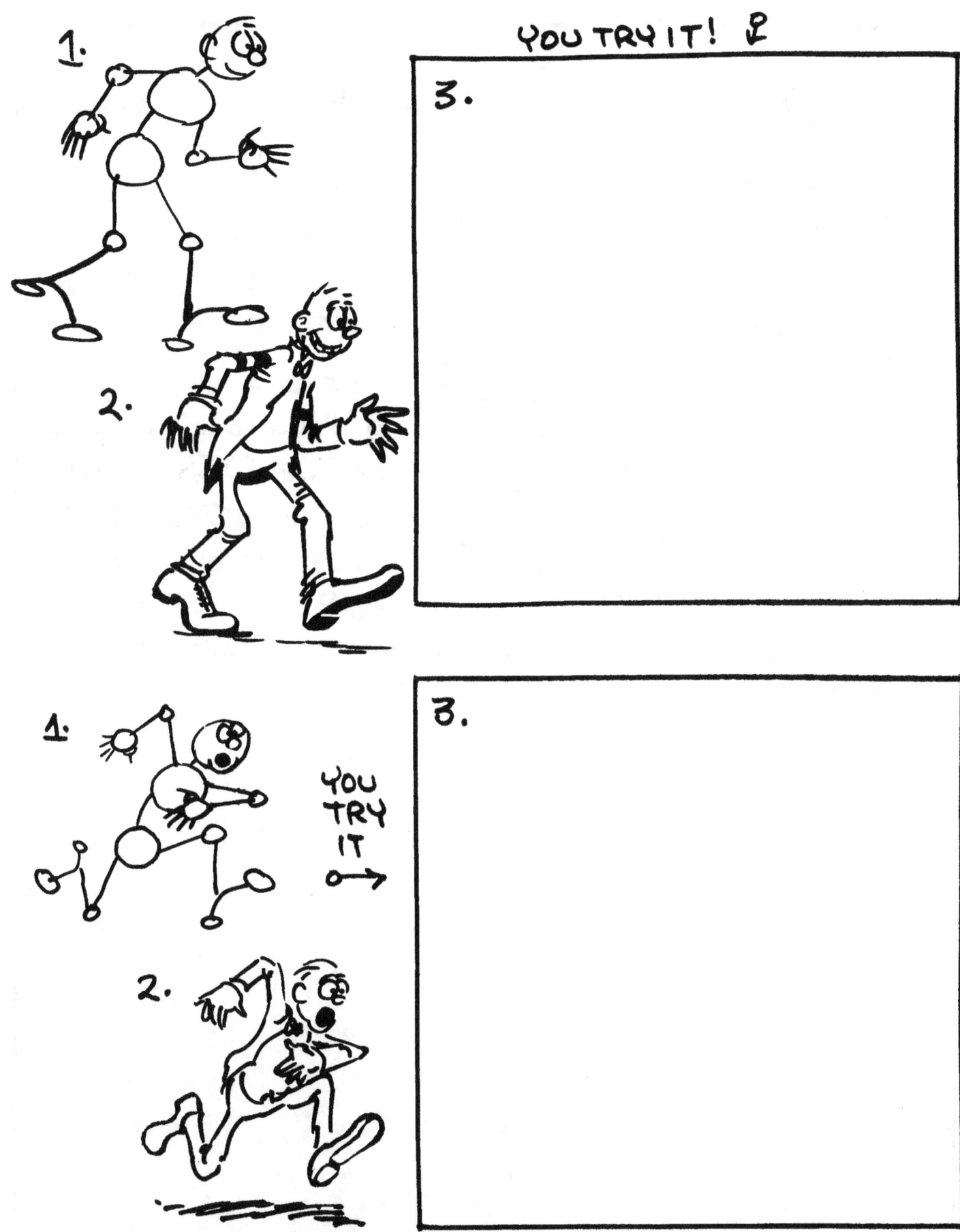

1.

2.

3.

YOU
TRY
IT →

1.

2.

3.

THE BAREFOOT SWIMMER

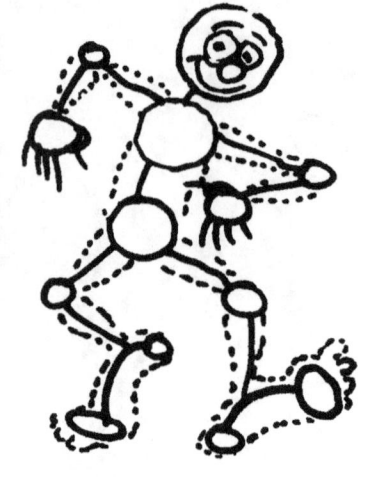

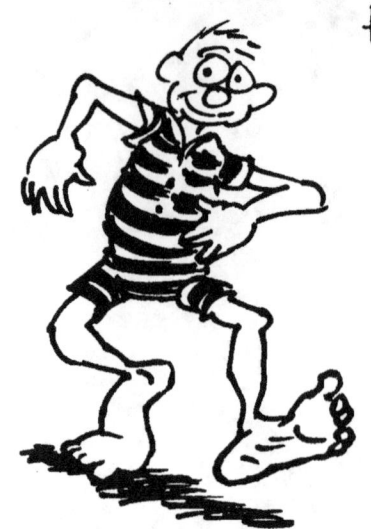

REMEMBER.. THE **INSTEP** OF THE FOOT DIPS INWARD FOLLOWING THE CURVE OF THE FOOT SPRING BONE. THE **OUTSIDE** OF THE FOOT IS FLAT. THE **BIG TOE** IS SEPARATED FROM THE LITTLE TOES. AND LIKE FINGERS, THE TOES CLUMP TOGETHER IN PAIRS.. NOW.. DRAW IN THE SPACE BELOW

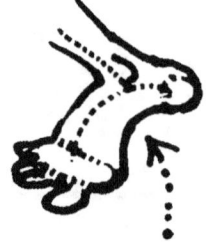

INSTEP

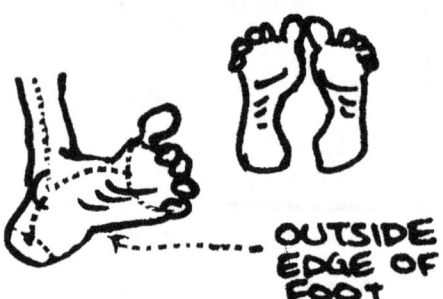

OUTSIDE EDGE OF FOOT

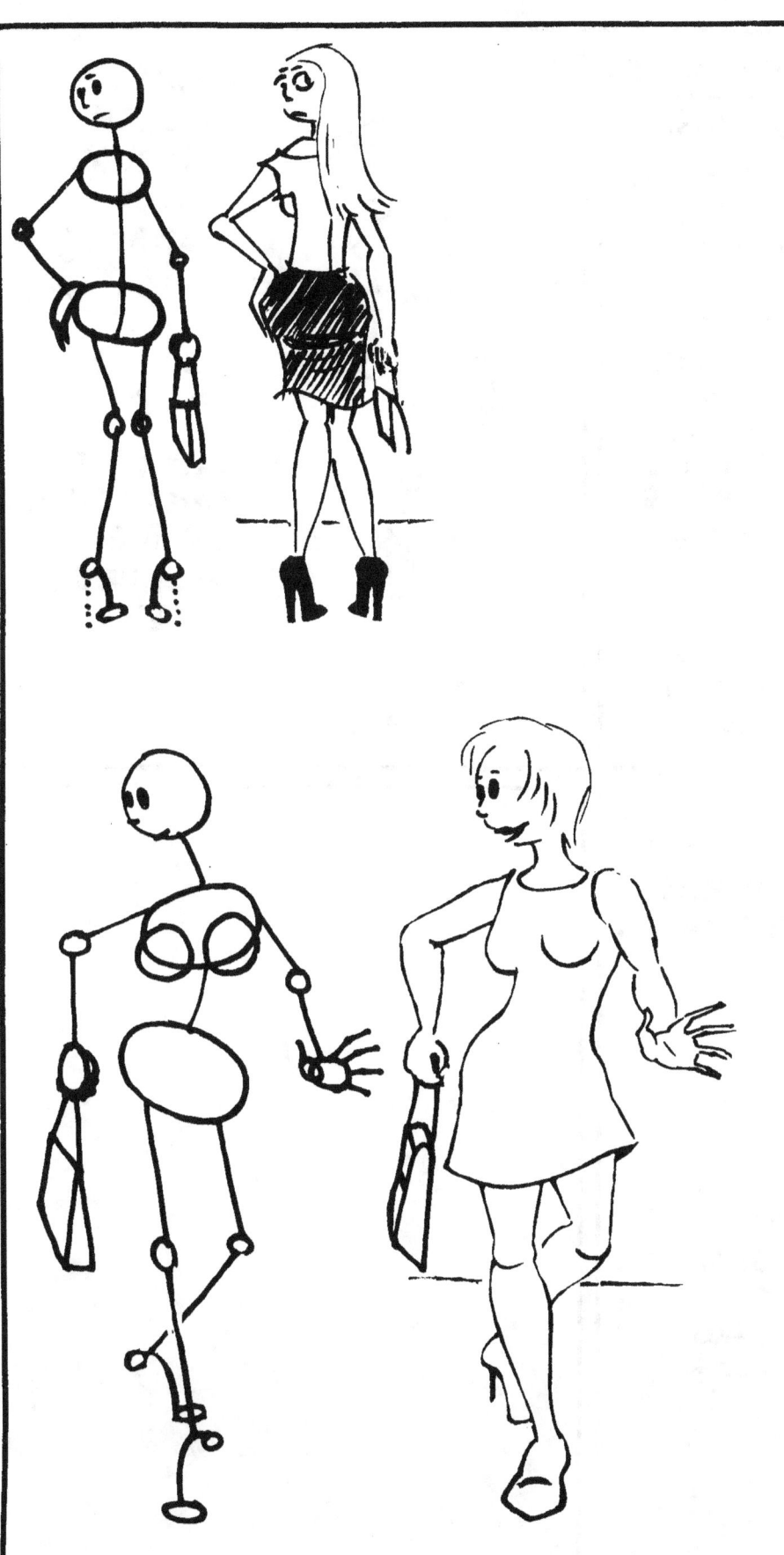

DRAW US..
KEEPING IN
MIND, THE
PRINCIPLES OF
FORESHORTENING,
WRAPAROUND
LINES, SIZE AND
OVERLAPPING.

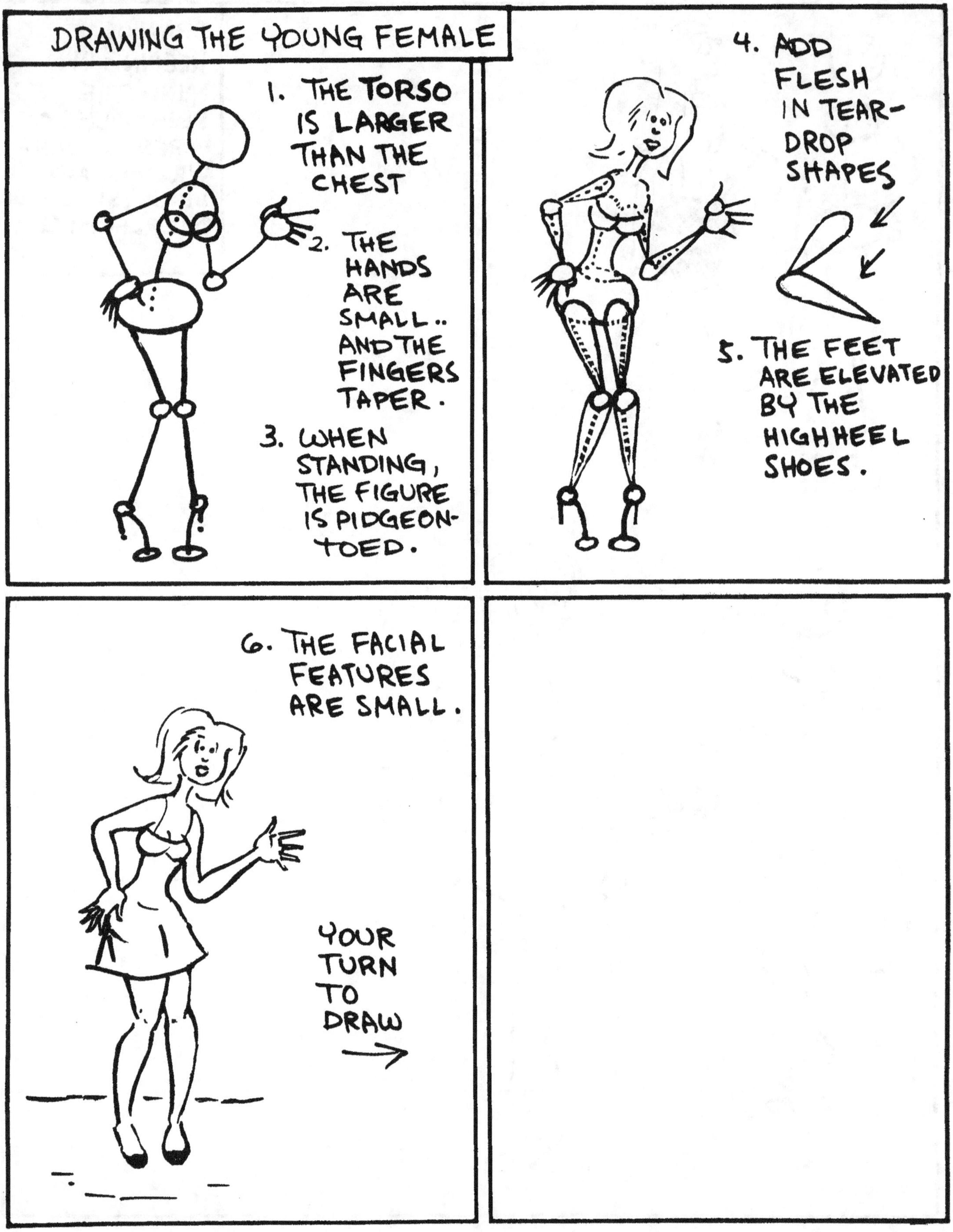

DRAWING THE YOUNG FEMALE

1. THE **TORSO** IS LARGER THAN THE CHEST

2. THE HANDS ARE SMALL.. AND THE FINGERS TAPER.

3. WHEN STANDING, THE FIGURE IS PIDGEON-TOED.

4. ADD FLESH IN TEAR-DROP SHAPES

5. THE FEET ARE ELEVATED BY THE HIGH HEEL SHOES.

6. THE FACIAL FEATURES ARE SMALL.

YOUR TURN TO DRAW →

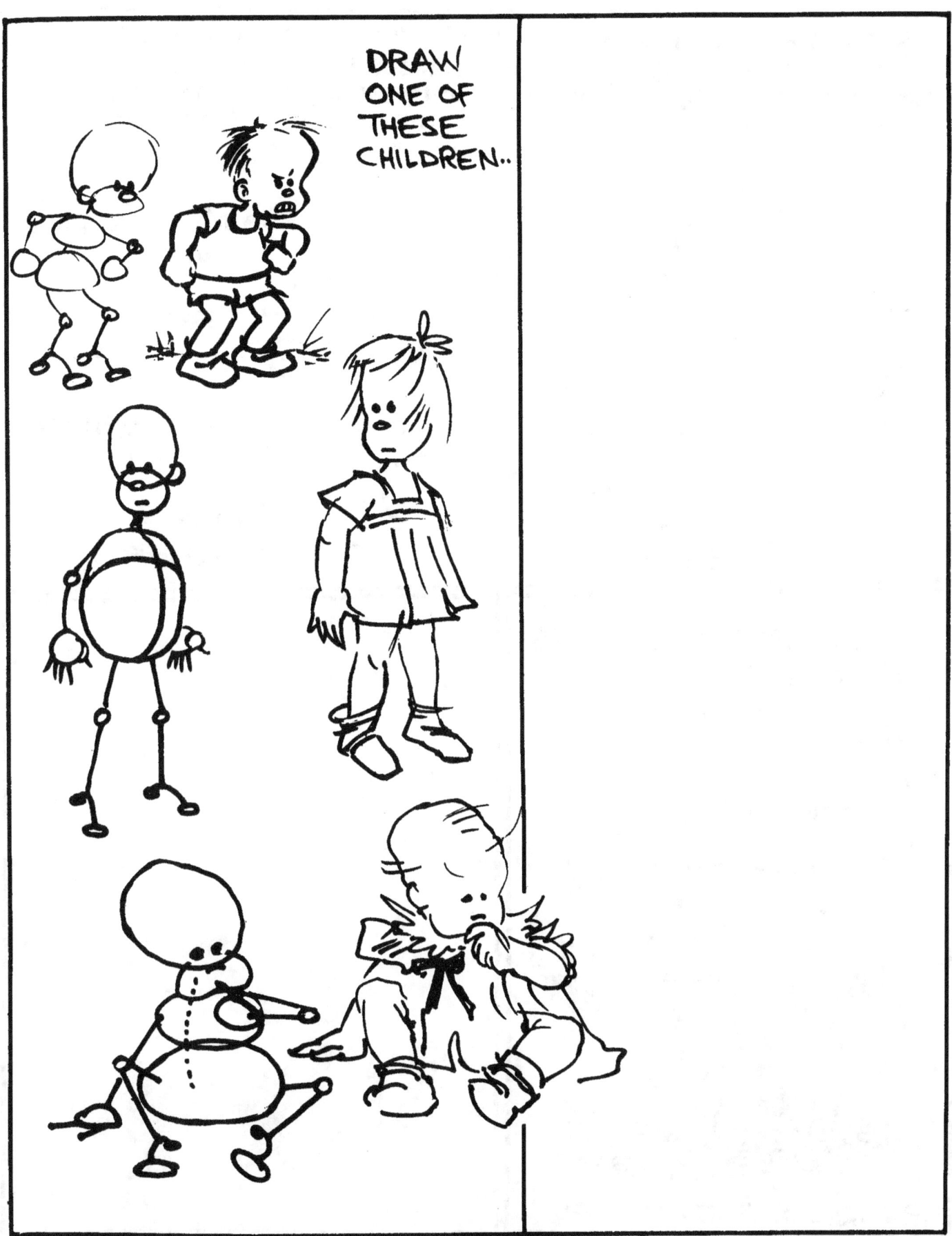

THE ANIMAL HAS A SIMILAR BONE STRUCTURE..BUT CERTAIN BONES ARE **SHORTENED**..THE SHINBONE ON THE BACK LEG.. AND THE **UPPER ARM** ON THE FRONT LEG (ARM)! THE **FOOT** BONE ON THE BACK LEG AND THE WRISTBONE ON THE FRONT LEG IS GREATLY **EXTENDED!**

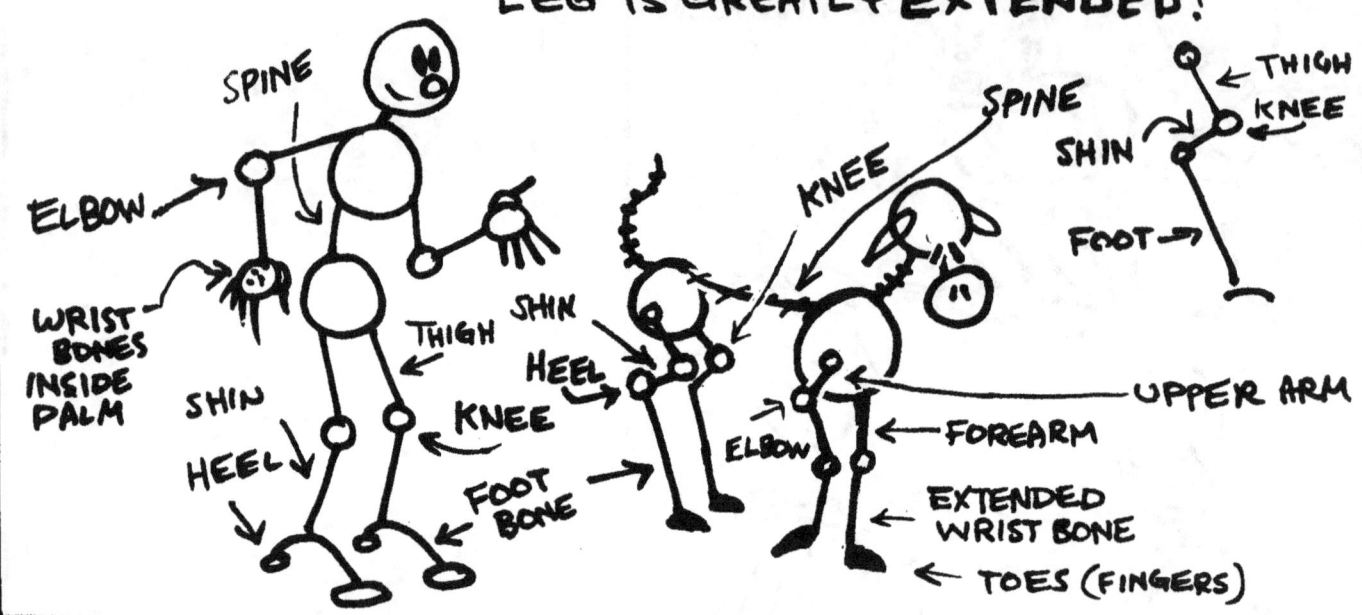

BUILD FLESH AND FEATURES AROUND THE SKELETON.. THE BACK LEG IS OFF THE GROUND ..

I'VE GOT A THORN IN MY FOOT!

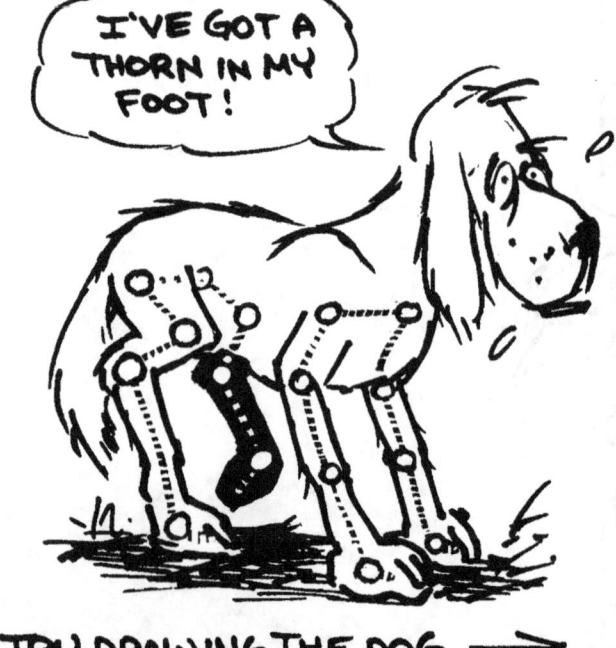

TRY DRAWING THE DOG ⟶

DETAIL – THE **6**TH PRINCIPLE OF PERSPECTIVE...

WE SEE SMALL **DETAILS** ON LARGE OBJECTS CLOSE TO US.. BUT THESE DETAILS DISAPPEAR AS THESE THINGS SHRINK IN THE DISTANCE. THE VEINS ON LEAVES AND **BARK** OF THE TREES.. THESE ARE DETAILS.

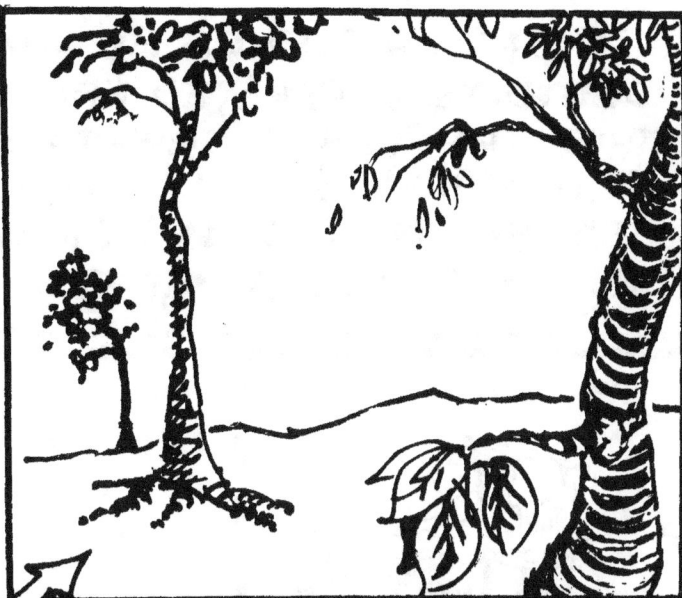

DRAW ONE OF THESE FORESTS

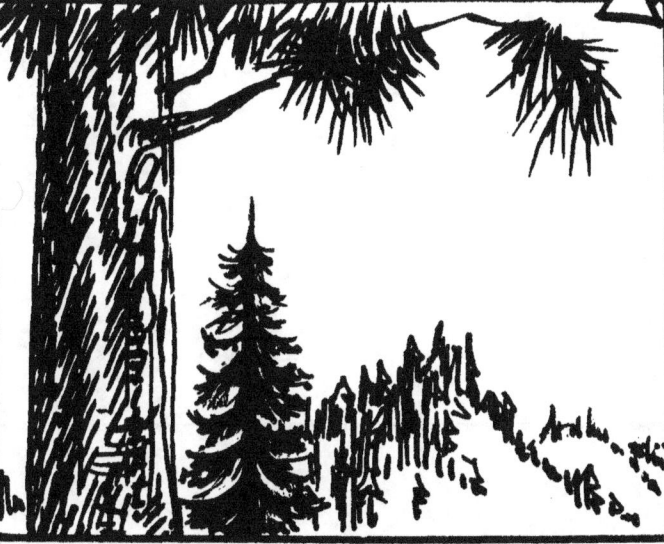

..AND NOW DRAW THE BED OF MUSHROOMS..

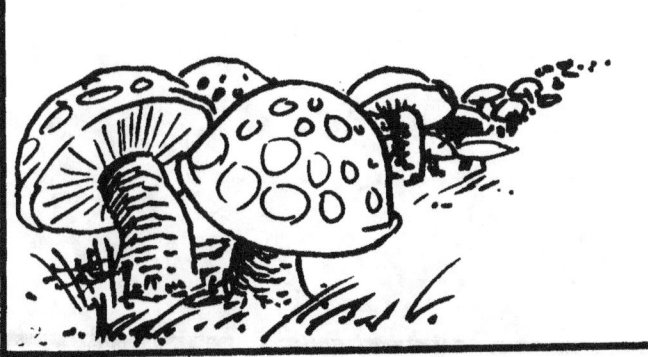

THE FOUR SCENES BELOW CONSIST OF THE **SAME** OBJECTS SEPARATED FROM EACH OTHER BY DISTANCE. THE ILLUSION IS CREATED BY **SIZE** AND **DETAIL** PRIMARILY! SMALL DETAILS ARE VISIBLE IN THE FOREGROUND **ONLY**! DRAW ANY **TWO** OF THESE SCENES IN THE SPACE PROVIDED.

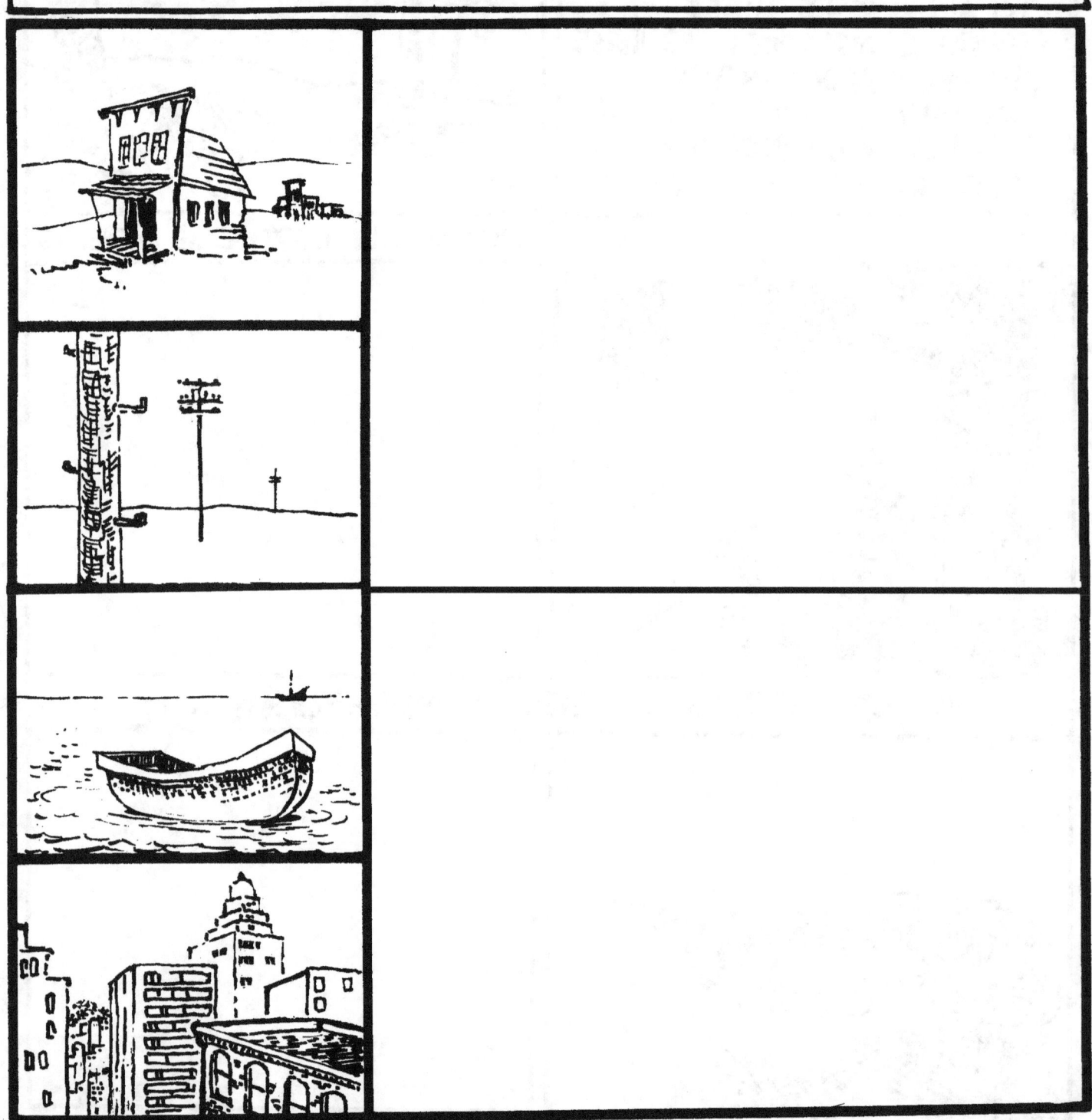

WELL.. THIS IS THE END OF THE BOOK..   IF YOU FOLLOWED THE DIRECTIONS, YOU CAN NOW DRAW.   SO.. **DRAW!!** PRACTICE AND EXPERIMENT WITH THESE PRINCIPLES OF ILLUSION... AND HAVE **FUN** BECAUSE THAT'S WHAT DRAWING IS.. **FUN!!**

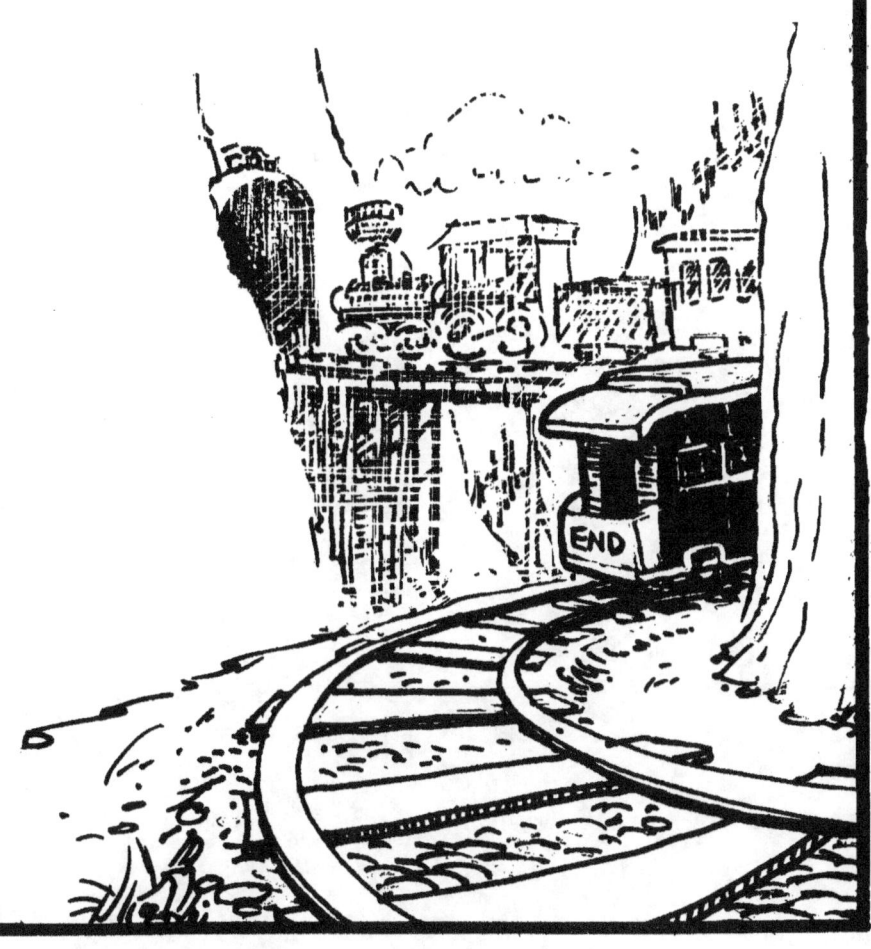